FINANCIAL MANAGEMENT OF FOREIGN EXCHANGE

An Operational Technique to Reduce Risk

FINANCIAL MANAGEMENT OF FOREIGN EXCHANGE

An Operational Technique to Reduce Risk

Bernard A. Lietaer

The M.I.T. Press
Cambridge, Massachusetts, and London, England

To my parents

Contents

Acknowledgments

The research presented in this book is a result of my successive contact with three environments. The academic circles provided the theory that forms the backbone of this work, a corporate environment the impulse to make it operational, and my present employer the time and support to prepare a publishable version of the results. During this process, I have accumulated substantial debts which I gladly acknowledge.

First, I would like to take this opportunity to thank very personally Professor Richard D. Robinson of the Massachusetts Institute of Technology for his continuous encouragement and assistance throughout my studies. I would like to express also my gratitude to Professor Gerald Pogue, Professor Charles P. Kindleberger, and Professor Eli Shapiro for their cooperation and suggestions. I owe my initiation to large computer systems, such as the Quadratic Programming System, to the benevolent advice of Mr. Richard Karash.

The theoretical model became an operational tool for actual financial management under the impulse and encouragement of a group of corporate financial officers. Therefore, I express my appreciation to Mr. Newton Hoyt, Mr. Angus Scott-Fleming, Mr. George Vickers, and Mr. Bob Kirby.

The preparation of a publishable version of this research became possible only through the time and support made available by the executives of my present employer, Cresap, McCormick and Paget Inc. I would like to thank especially Mr. Richard M. Paget, Mr. Albert Kushner, and Mr. George M. Whitmore. Finally, I am very grateful to Miss Ila Shaw and Mr. Joseph Roberts for the excellent editing work performed on the manuscript.

Mexico City BERNARD A. LIETAER
May 1970

1
Introduction

1.1 Objectives and Plan

The literature on foreign exchange has been very prolific on implications of various types of crises for governments or central banks. The causes, remedies, and techniques of international monetary adjustments have been favorite topics of many economists over recent years. Governments are almost overwhelmed with advice on how to handle currency instabilities. In contrast, what a corporation should do in view of a foreign-exchange crisis has been met by a virtual silence from the academic world. In most international corporations, an atmosphere of panic reigns when the value of a major currency is readjusted. A last-minute estimate of potential losses and some emergency financial juggling are typical reactions. What has long been needed by the treasurers of international companies is a systematic and analytical approach to the problems arising from a foreign-exchange crisis.

The first and major objective of this book is to meet this need by developing an *operationally effective* technique to determine international finance strategies taking into account currency fluctuations. "Operationally effective" entails two requirements: (1) The technique has to be usable by present-day firms, and (2) It has to represent a measurable improvement over existing practices.

The data requirements for the technique are expressed in financial terms, understandable to financial officers who are dealing with the problem. These data are available in most current information systems of large international corporations. Also, large corporations have access to the relatively powerful computers required to handle this technique. The tests of the model have been carried out on an IBM 360/65 with a model 360/45 input-output computer. The largest test was resolved on an IBM 360/75. Some of the refinements explained in this book could of course be scaled down to meet more modest needs and means.

Finally, the best guarantee that this technique is usable is that it actually solved hedging problems for a billion-dollar company in New York.

The effectiveness of the method has been tested under actual conditions. Over a recent 16-month period, financing and hedging against devaluation of Brazilian cruzeiros cost one major U.S. corporation $1.6 million. It was subsequently shown that had the treasurer been guided by optimal solutions arrived at by the computerized technique he could have reduced the costs to $275,000, a saving of 83%. Improvements on current practices can thus be measured precisely with this technique.

By far the most frequent type of foreign-exchange crisis is a devaluation. The technique is therefore developed and illustrated for the case of a devaluation. The adaptations to revaluations and other types of international monetary systems will be explained in Chapter 9.

One of the first applications of management science to the field of international finance is described in this book; the approach is resolutely analytical and differs from the majority of international financial management handbooks which are often purely descriptive. However, the use of mathematical or specialized language is avoided wherever possible. The mathematics required in Chapters 2, 3, and 9 includes only high school algebra and introductory courses in operations research and statistical decision theory.

The book's plan is as follows: This introductory chapter summarizes all the preliminary facts and concepts necessary to understand the problem and the theoretical model. In Chapters 2 and 3, the theoretical model is formally presented. Some examples, of increasing complexity, explain the major characteristics of the unitemporal and multitemporal models. A case study on a hypothetical "Ace International Corporation" shows how the model handles "real-life" financial transactions and operational constraints. Chapter 4 presents all the elements of the Ace International case; in Chapter 5, the solution is given and discussed. Chapters 6 and 7 explain how the basic model used in the Ace International case can be built on, by refining some assumptions and eliminating some simplifications. In Chapter 8, the practical implementation of the model in a corporate environment is presented.

The devaluation-hedging technique developed in all the previous chapters is adapted in Chapter 9 to revaluations, speculations, and a variety of crises under new monetary systems. Chapter 9 is included to prevent the outdating of the technique should the present world monetary system be modified.

Finally, in Chapter 10, directions for future research are suggested.

1.2 The Problem

For many large international companies, hedging against currency devaluation is becoming an important function of the international finance department. A short survey of some of the larger international companies in New York reveals that devaluation risk is considered the major problem in their international financial operations.

Parity modifications are not exceptional events. A recent study[1] reveals that 96 of the 109 currencies about which data have been gathered from the end of 1948 to the end of 1967 devalued at least once. Table 1.1[2] gives some information on the numbers of these devaluations per currency.

TABLE 1.1 Devaluation Frequency in 109 Currencies (End of 1948 to End of 1967)

Appreciation	1
No devaluation	12
One devaluation	27
Two devaluations	24
Three devaluations	24
Frequent devaluations	21
Total	109

The currencies that were devalued twice during this period include those of some major countries: United Kingdom, Austria, India, Greece, Ghana, Ceylon, Ireland, New Zealand, Denmark, and the United Arab Republic. The French franc is among the currencies that were devalued three times within the period. Even more numerous were devaluations for countries with multiple exchange rates, including Bolivia, China, Paraguay, Thailand, Yugoslavia, Argentina, Brazil, Chile, Colombia, and Uruguay.

These statistics give only a partial idea of the frequency with which devaluation problems are faced by a corporate treasurer. Simply stating that the British pound experienced two devaluations since World War II does not give an accurate idea of the number of crises this currency experienced. During the late fifties, throughout the

1. Margaret G. de Vries, "The Magnitude of Exchange Devaluation," *Finance and Development*, vol. 5, no. 2 (June 1968), pp. 8–12.
2. Ibid., p. 11.

sixties, and up to November 18, 1967, approximately a dozen false alarms kept the corporate treasurer uneasy about his sterling trans- actions. The statistics on the number of actual devaluations understate dramatically the frequency with which a treasurer has to solve devaluation hedging problems.

Another measure of the importance of hedging — or the protection of income and investment against devaluation — is the amount of money a company can lose if no adequate hedging is performed. The statistics on the actual devaluation amounts throw some light on that aspect of the problem:

What is often not fully realized is that for 62 countries the magnitude of postwar devaluation exceeded 40 per cent. Some 38 countries have devalued between 40 and 75 per cent; this includes not only the United Kingdom and Ireland, which have devalued just over 40 per cent in total, but also Austria, Finland, India, Mexico, New Zealand, Peru, the Philippines, and Turkey, which have devalued by larger amounts.

For another 24 countries, devaluation has gone beyond 75 per cent. Among European countries in this group are France, Greece, Iceland, Spain, and Yugoslavia. Other countries devaluing by these large amounts have been seven Latin American countries (Argentina, Bolivia, Brazil, Columbia, Chile, Paraguay, and Uruguay), as well as Ghana, Indonesia, Israel, Korea and Vietnam.[3]

Most of the examples given in this book relate to Latin America, where the problem is most acute, but the technique as developed in these pages is clearly relevant to all continents and to the vast majority of countries, including the major powers. A large international company is perpetually dealing to some extent in devaluation-prone currencies.

What are the problems that a devaluation creates for a corporation? A look at some annual reports will help to answer this question.

The 1967 consolidated annual report of the Hoover Company states that

the estimated net losses resulting from the 1967 devaluation of British, Finnish and Danish currencies, less applicable income taxes, amounted to $6,891,508.

These losses represented 55¢ per share of net income to be deducted from the total net income of $2.03 per share.

Eastman Kodak Company reports:

as the result of foreign currency devaluation . . . losses amounted to $2.5 million in 1968, as against $9.5 million in 1967 — of which $8.7 million resulted from the devaluation of the British pound and related currencies.

3. Ibid., p. 9.

International Telephone and Telegraph Corporation reported in 1967

extraordinary losses of $3.2 million applicable to the devaluation of
the English pound and the Spanish peseta. . . .

In its report to stockholders in December 1967, The Firestone Tire
& Rubber Co. disclosed that

foreign currency devaluation deducted from income amounted to
$6.5 million this year (1967) and $4.2 million last year (1966). The devaluation
of the British pound sterling on November 18, 1967, and other affected
currencies resulted in no loss to the Company.

The European subsidiary of Xerox Corporation, by contrast, reported
a profit of almost $4.4 million on the British pound crisis of 1967.

These losses, or profits, result from writing off the net exposure by
the amount of the devaluation. Net exposure — the difference between
exposed assets and exposed liabilities — is the key variable in devaluation hedging. It warrants, therefore, a thorough discussion.

An exposed asset or liability is an asset or liability the dollar value
of which is affected by a devaluation. For instance, accounts receivable
in a foreign currency, when translated into dollars, will be written off
by the amount of the devaluation, as shown in the following example:
Sales per 100 million pesos were recorded at the exchange rate of
100 pesos to the dollar. The resulting accounts receivable are recorded
in the headquarters as $1 million. The peso devalues to 125 pesos to
the dollar; the collection of accounts receivable still yields 100 million
pesos, if no bad debts occur. But when these receipts are exchanged for
dollars, only $800,000 have been collected. Hence, the devaluation loss
amounts to $200,000.

Accounts receivable in foreign currency are the most obvious kind
of exposed assets. Bank deposits, cash, and all other current assets
expressed in local currency are similarly vulnerable. Exposed assets,
however, are only one side of the coin. An exposed liability, such as
a bank loan in local currency, will react inversely to a devaluation.
For example, since fewer dollars will be required to pay back a loan in
pesos after a devaluation, a devaluation profit would be realized.

Some assets or liabilities cannot be readily classified as completely
exposed or unexposed: The most important example is inventories.
(In Chapter 4, a technique to evaluate the percentage of exposure of
inventories is presented.) Once all exposed assets and liabilities are
determined, the corporation can compute its net exposure, which is the
total amount on which devaluation losses could occur. The Hoover
Company, Eastman Kodak Company, and International Telephone
and Telegraph Corporation all had a positive net exposure in November

1967; such exposure resulted in the heavy losses reported earlier. Firestone Tire & Rubber Co. was perfectly hedged against the British pound devaluation; in other words, its net exposure was zero. In contrast, Xerox Corporation had a substantial negative net exposure in November 1967; such exposure amounts in fact to a speculative position in pounds sterling.

It is important to note that the net exposure as defined here differs from usual accounting concepts. The Accounting Research Bulletin, No. 45, defines net exposure as net current assets (short-term assets minus short-term liabilities). This method usually overstates real devaluation losses. In comparison, the National Accounting Association states in its publication, No. 36, that net exposure is net financially denominated assets. This method tends to understate devaluation losses.

Hedging, or the control of the net exposure, is a complex operation because of 4 major difficulties: (1) the inseparability of financing and hedging; (2) the unreliability of forecast costs; (3) timing; and (4) foreign exchange controls.

1. In solving a devaluation-hedging problem on a rational basis, the first difficulty is that hedging cannot be considered apart from financing, because the necessity of meeting cash requirements in a foreign subsidiary is directly related to the net exposure of the operation. The net exposure is changed by the use of local bank loans, imported dollars, or a financial swap to meet financing requirements. Thus, the problems of financing and hedging cannot be solved independently.

2. Cost implications are also relevant, because different financing sources have different costs and such costs can be predicted with only variable certainty. For example, a local bank loan in Brazil has an effective annual interest cost of from 20% to 45%, and sometimes even higher.[4] On the other hand, a dollar loan in the United States can be obtained at 6% to 10%, and these funds can be exchanged into local currency. However, foreign and U.S. financing sources differ by more than their effective interest cost. A local loan will decrease the exposure of the subsidiary, while a straight dollar loan from the United States will not modify it. Therefore, in choosing between the two sources, one must take into account the probability and possible amount of a devaluation during the period in which these loans will be outstanding.

---

4. Bank loans were noted at 74% effective annual interest cost in Brazil. The legal maximum is 12%, but compensating balance, prepayment of interest charges, and special transaction costs multiply the real cost.

If the probability and amount of devaluation are high, the local loan at 45% may be preferable to the straight dollar loan at 6%.

The comparative unpredictability of these costs is also a relevant factor. The risk of large errors in a forecast cost in New York is obviously smaller than in Brazil or the Philippines. If a specific sum is critically needed 6 months from now, it is less risky to rely on straight dollar loans than on local bank loans.

3. Timing is another major complication in the protection of working capital in devaluation-prone currencies. Ideally, one should hedge completely the day before a devaluation, and, from the day after, no coverage costs should be incurred, but this theoretical technique is irrelevant for two reasons. First, it is rare that a devaluation date is known with certainty. Devaluation timing is usually a well-kept secret, because the government, to make the devaluation successful, must surprise the business community and speculators as much as possible, Second, the availability of hedging possibilities varies with time. In most cases when a devaluation is imminent, forward-exchange contracts and short-term local loans either simply disappear from the market or their cost rises astronomically.

For these two reasons — the uncertainty about the timing of a devaluation and the instability of the cost of hedging — one cannot rely on emergency measures just before a devaluation. A medium-term loan decision made now can and does affect the exposure many months hence. The timing of forward-exchange contracts is even more critical. Hopefully, the devaluation will occur in a period when the net exposure is minimal. In other words, the treasurer, when making his financial and hedging decisions, has to take into account not only costs and exposure effects but also the maturities of each of the alternatives he is considering.

4. The final elements that complicate the treasurer's decisions are foreign-exchange controls. Limitations on profit repatriation, multiple exchange rates, and restrictions on the availability of swaps or forward-exchange contracts are typical regulations the treasurer has to take into account.

1.3 The Solution Technique: A Qualitative Description

The aim of this section is to give a qualitative feeling of how the solution technique tackles the problem. A formal description of the mathematical model follows in Chapters 2, 3, and 4. The stress, at this point, will be on the general structure of the problem, or how the different aspects of the problem are interconnected within the same general solution technique.

The problem can be seen to contain 3 elements: expected costs, strategy risk, and operational constraints. *The whole problem can be described as an attempt to find a combination of financing and hedging operations (i.e., a hedging strategy) that minimizes expected costs and strategy risk and does not violate any of the operational constraints.* A brief description of the problem's three elements follows:

1. *Expected costs.* One aim of the hedging problem solution is to minimize the costs involved in the operation. Expected costs are of two types: The first type is the expense arising out of all the financing and hedging operations. This would be reduced, for example, by the interest yield on bonds in which excess cash has been invested. The second type of expected cost is the expected devaluation loss. This loss depends on the probability of a devaluation, the amount of the expected devaluation and the net exposure.

2. *Strategy risk.* The second aim of the hedging problem solution is to reduce the overall strategy risk of the financial operations involved. Strategy risk is a combination of two types of risk. The "business risk" measures the risk generated from relying on future financing and hedging possibilities whose costs are not known with certainty. All uncertainty other than devaluation would be included as business risk. The second strategy risk, "the devaluation risk," is a combination of risks arising from the possibility of wrong estimates in devaluation probabilities and devaluation amounts.

3. *Operational constraints.* These are the large and complex set of operational requirements, policy decisions, and legal constraints in the context of which the problem has to be solved. Examples of operational requirements are the financial requirements for each period in the planning horizon. Financial requirements have to be met by new funds from whatever source (receipts, local loans, swaps, dollar loans, and so forth). In addition, the deposits and interest expenses on the decisions within the planning period have to be budgeted. A policy decision might determine the minimum balances of local bank loans that would keep the lines of credit open, or the specific levels of some financial ratios. Availability of swaps or forward-exchange contracts, balance sheet covenants for some loan agreements, and foreign-exchange controls are examples of legal constraints. The solution chosen by the treasurer cannot violate any of these operational constraints.

Before undertaking a description of the problem in mathematical terms, one must consider the question: How can risk be measured? Risk is here initially defined as the uncertainty of the exact outcome of an event. The larger the spread of a devaluation level, or a cost, taken in a given period, the larger the variance, or risk.

In this book, risk is evaluated by a measure of the dispersion of the potential outcome around the expected outcome: This measure is called the variance. The mathematical relationship between maximum spreads and variances will be given in following sections. It is important to note here that a combination of 2 variances requires introduction of the squares of the variables involved. The function we want to minimize, then, or the objective function, will be composed of 2 parts:

$$\text{minimize } Z = \text{expected cost} + \text{risk}.$$

Since the cost evaluation will be a linear equation and the risk factors will be expressed in quadratic terms, the solution technique will have a quadratic objective function; that is, it is quadratic programming.[5]

It is also important to note that there is not one optimal solution to the devaluation hedging problem but an infinite set of optimal solutions. At one extreme of the solution spectrum, there is the minimum risk solution. This corresponds to a solution in which risk has been minimized at any price. Obviously, this strategy corresponds to a very expensive solution. At the other extreme, there is a solution that is concerned only with minimizing costs, regardless of the risk involved. Between these 2 extremes, a theoretically infinite set of solutions exists with an increasing weight on cost reduction at the expense of risk avoidance. The objective function will be optimized for all different weights given to risk and costs. That is, our problem becomes:

$$\text{minimize } Z = L \text{ (expected cost)} + \text{(risk)},$$

where L will vary from zero (for a complete risk avoider) to infinity (for a complete gambler). In other words, this is a parametric quadratic programming problem.[6]

These solutions are all optimal,[7] in the sense that each represents the best solution possible for a specific kind of temperament. The complete risk avoider is willing to pay almost any price to escape risk; the gambler is ready to take large risks for an additional cost saving. Most treasurers making a hedging decision are likely to lie between these two extremes. The best way to choose the optimal solution for a specific treasurer is to use his risk preference curves, as will be explained in a

5. George Bernard Dantzig, *Linear Programming and Extensions* (Princeton, N. J.: Princeton University Press, 1963), Sections 24–29, pp. 496–497.
6. The computer code used in the solution of this model is an updated version of program RS QPF4, Share No. 3326. It has been adapted to the IBM 360/65 by Mr. Richard Karash.
7. Technically, a solution is optimal if no other solution with the same cost has a lower risk, or no other solution with the same risk has a lower cost.

later chapter. The personal trade-off between the risk and the expected costs to avoid the risk is therefore taken into account.

The data inputs required for a solution of the problem (see Figure 1.1)

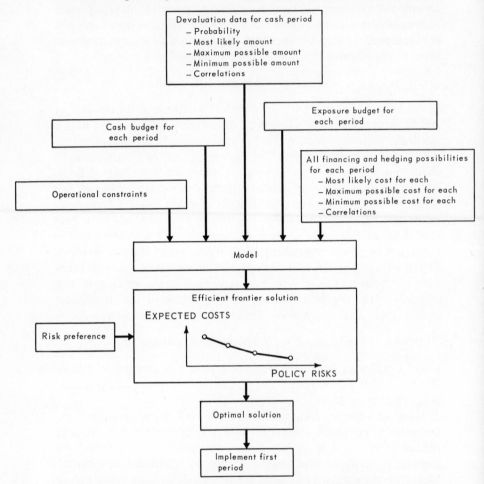

FIGURE 1.1   Inputs and Outputs of the Model

must now be considered. The first step is to determine a planning horizon. The length of the planning horizon depends on a large number of factors: necessity, maturity periods of the decisions involved, and reliability of the forecast over time. After the planning horizon is determined, the time unit is chosen: days, weeks, months, or quarters. For instance, if one chooses a three-quarters projection, with monthly time units, he has 9 months, or periods, in the model.

The second step is to forecast for each month the probabilities of a devaluation, the devaluation amount, and the spread of this amount. Several recent books are devoted to refining the art of devaluation forecasting.[8] But this remains an art, and no other forecast method exists but conjecture, more or less sophisticated. The model takes into account the 3 monthly parameters mentioned. It also takes into account the effect of errors in estimates for any specific month on the estimates for other months.[9] This latter effect is an important ingredient in the total strategy risk. For instance, the total risk will be lower when an error in the devaluation probability estimate of a specific month does not affect the other estimates than when an error in one month forces a revision of the estimates of all the future months. In summary, devaluation estimation inputs are of four types: devaluation probability, possible devaluation amount, possible spread of the amount, and the effect of an error in the devaluation estimates on all the later months' estimates.

The third set of required data is a cash budget for each month in the planning horizon. This cash budget describes the financing requirements expected in each month before interest cost and deposits needed to meet these requirements.

The fourth data set consists of all the possible alternative sources of financing and hedging available. The expected cost, the possible spread of these costs, and the expected amounts available within this spread have to be forecast. The degree to which the costs depend on each other is also a relevant factor. For example, the costs of all bank loans tend to rise and fall concurrently in response to the capital market conditions. Correlation estimates of the costs of financing and hedging operations will take this element into account. A final set of constraints represents the legal limitations and policy decisions that cannot be violated by the optimal solution.

Chapter 4 describes a case study dealing with all these data and shows how they are included in the model.

After the parametric quadratic programming problem has been solved, the output consists of a set of optimal solutions, each corresponding to a given level of risk (that is, each with a given value of parameter L). Each optimal solution is a listing of how much of each financing and hedging possibility should be used in each period. The total expected cost and risk of the strategy are also computed.

8. For example, Paul Einzig, *Leads and Lags: the Main Cause of Devaluation* (New York: St. Martins Press, 1968). Also, Paul Einzig, *Foreign Exchange Crisis: An Essay in Economic Pathology* (New York: St. Martins Press, 1968).
9. Measured by the covariance of devaluation probabilities and amounts over time.

Management has to choose what level of risk it is ready to assume during this planning period (for instance, by defining its risk preference curves) and this level determines which optimal solution is best adapted to management's needs.

Only the financing and hedging decision of the first period should be implemented. If new data are made available before the second period, sensitivity analysis can be made on the present optimal solution for the second month. If the effect of the information on the present optimal solution is important, the problem can be resolved in the beginning of the second month. The process then starts all over again.

1.4   Some Remarks on Risk

The literature on the subject makes a distinction between *risk* and *uncertainty*.[10] A problem involves risk when all the possible outcomes and their probabilities are known. Coin flipping or Russian roulette are examples of risky situations. Uncertainty is involved when all the possible outcomes are not known or when the probabilities of all the possible outcomes are not known. The latter case is usually solved by assuming that a risk situation can approximate the uncertainty problem. This distinction between risk and uncertainty is, therefore, irrelevant for practical purposes.

1.4.1   *The Measure of Risk*

Risk or uncertainty in business circles may mean a host of different things, including the probability of losing a certain amount of dollars, the chance of a bankruptcy, the different possible outcomes of a contract or financial operation, or the variability of earnings. Risk is defined in this book as variability of earnings or costs.

Variability, or volatility, of earnings or costs reflects the range in which earnings or costs of a specific transaction or strategy can move. A measure of variability, or of risk under our definition, is the variance. The variance of a random variable $\tilde{X}$ is the second moment about the mean,

$$\text{variance of } \tilde{X} = V(\tilde{X}) = E[\tilde{X} - E(\tilde{X})]^2,$$

where $E(\tilde{X})$ means the expected value of $\tilde{X}$. Also, the square root of the variance is the standard deviation of the random variable.

A financial transaction is considered risky if its actual costs can vary widely, that is, if the variance of its cost is high. Similarly, a high-risk

10. Donald F. Farrar, *The Investment Decision under Uncertainty* (Englewood Cliffs, N. J.: Prentice Hall, 1962).

financing and hedging strategy is a combination of transactions whose total cost or return (including devaluation losses) is predictable only within a wide range. A larger variance is therefore associated with wider range and, in nonmathematical terms, a higher risk.

By using a variance as measure of risk, it is necessary to express all the probability distributions of the model in terms of two-parameter distributions. This limitation is not very important, because the family of two-parameter distributions allows for a wide variety of shapes.

Most of the probability distributions in this book are assumed to be normal distributions, because they are the most familiar probability distribution in the literature, and the estimating procedure is thereby simplified.

Intuitively meaningful quantities can be converted into estimates of the expected value and the variance. These quantities are the most likely value, Z, the highest possible value A, and the lowest possible value B. From these three estimates, classical formulas give estimations of the expected value $E = [2Z + (A + B)/2]/3$ and the variance $V = [(B - A)/6]^2$.

Similarly, from a variance, probability estimates can be deduced. The standard deviation (square root of the variance) is a convenient yardstick for probability estimates (see Figure 1.2). The probability

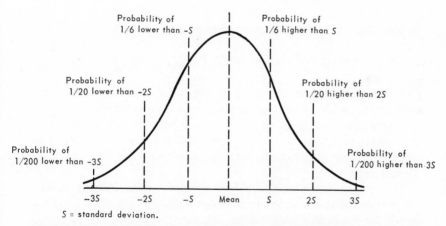

Probability of
1/6 lower than -S

Probability of
1/6 higher than S

Probability of
1/20 lower than -2S

Probability of
1/20 higher than 2S

Probability of
1/200 lower than -3S

Probability of
1/200 higher than 3S

-3S   -2S   -S   Mean   S   2S   3S

S = standard deviation.

FIGURE 1.2   Probability Estimates from Normal Distributions

that the random variable will be further than 1 standard deviation from the mean is 1/6 on each side. In other words, two-thirds of the time the random variable will be within 1 standard deviation S from the mean. The probability that the random variable is 2 standard deviations from the mean is only 1/20 on each side, and the corresponding value for 3 standard deviations is 1/200. Therefore, if a hedging strategy has a $100 expected cost and a variance of 100, there is 1 chance out of 6 that the costs will be larger than $110 and 1 chance out of 20 that they will go beyond $120. Only with a probability of 1/200 could they exceed the $130 mark.

The assumption of normal distributions is not a requirement for the model. Any two-parameter distributions can be handled. Even when normal distributions are not used, a weaker probability statement can be used to give intuitively meaningful measures of risk. Chebyshev's inequality states that the probability that a deviation from the mean will exceed a given value e is smaller than the quantity variance/e^2, for example,

$$\text{probability } (|\tilde{x} - \text{mean}| \geq e) \leq \text{variance}/e^2.$$

After dropping the normality assumption, the previous example of a $100 expected cost and a variance of 100 becomes:

$$\text{probability } (|\tilde{x} - 100| \geq 30) \leq 100/30^2 = 1/9.$$

In other words, the probability that costs are higher than $130 or lower than 70 is smaller than 1/9. In using this probability statement, one should keep in mind that the Chebyshev inequality is often very conservative, in the sense that the probabilities are likely to be much smaller than the upper boundary given by this inequality.

1.4.2 Theoretical Implications of the Use of a Variance as Measure of Risk

The use of a variance as measure of risk has several theoretical implications. One of the two following conditions must be satisfied: (1) either the devaluation hedging strategies have a normally distributed cost probability curve, or (2) the treasurer's risk preference curve must be quadratic. The justifications for this statement have been made in several papers.[11]

The first condition rarely holds in the devaluation hedging model: the cost distributions of the total hedging strategy are often bimodal, as will be shown in a later section.

Therefore the second condition becomes a practical necessity. The

11. John Lintner, "The Valuation of Risk Assets and the Selection of Risky Investments in Stock Portfolios and Capital Budgets," *Review of Economics and Statistics*, 47 (February 1965), pp. 13–37. Also, Harry M. Markowitz, *Portfolio Selection: Efficient Diversification of Investments*, Cowles Foundation Monograph No. 16 (New York: John Wiley & Sons, Inc., 1959).

requirements of quadratic risk preference curves means that the treasurer must be risk averse if the model is to be useful. He is more willing to risk a $1,000 loss with a probability of 50% than a loss of $50,000 with a probability of 1%. Other works have shown that the quadratic preference curve is not an unreasonable assumption for most people.[12] But the existing risk aversion of treasurers is in conflict with some recent developments in financial theory.

It is argued that the diversification of risk is far more efficient at the stockholder's level than at the company level. For example, a firm should not try to reduce its variability of earnings by purchasing other product lines; the stockholder, by diversifying his portfolio, can accomplish this task at lower costs. This argument is valid, but the optimization of the stockholders' wealth is not the only objective of a company. The financial officer is tempted to reduce the probability of a heavy loss for which he would be assumed responsible. Hence, risk aversion is a common pattern of the business community.

The aim of this book's devaluation-hedging model is to help the financial officer of a company to make decisions that fit his assumptions and risk preferences. Whether these assumptions and risk preferences are what they should be or not is another problem.

The concepts which are required to understand the problem and the theoretical model now have been presented. In the next two chapters, this model is developed and illustrated by some simple examples.

12. Richard A. Brealey, *An Introduction to Risk and Return From Common Stocks*, (Cambridge: The M.I.T. Press, 1969). Also, S. A. Ozga, *Expectations in Economic Theory*, (London: Weidenfeld and Nicolson, 1965).

2
The Unitemporal Model

A devaluation-hedging strategy is a set of financing and hedging transactions over time. It can be considered as a kind of portfolio of transactions. The devaluation-hedging model is an extension and adaptation of portfolio theory. Each financing and hedging transaction in this model plays the role of a security in portfolio theory. The hedging strategy, or combination of financing and hedging transactions, has a function equivalent to a portfolio. Two basic works of portfolio theory are the starting point of the devaluation-hedging model: the Markowitz covariance model and Sharpe's diagonal model.[1] These theories are extended to handle mixed probability distributions and multitemporal problems.

The financing and hedging transactions are expressed in the theoretical treatment by "exposed assets" or "exposed liabilities." Taking a loan in local currency is equivalent to acquiring an exposed liability. Investing in bonds denominated in local currency is a typical purchase of an exposed asset. In Chapter 4, it will be shown by the Ace International case study that all financing and hedging transactions can be handled as if they were exposed assets and liabilities or combinations of them.

The unitemporal model of this chapter is the primary building block of the devaluation-hedging model. The unitemporal model analyzes the problem as if only one time period were involved. In Chapter 3, the multitemporal model will incorporate as units a set of unitemporal models.

1. Harry M. Markowitz, "Portfolio Selection," *The Journal of Finance*, vol. 7, no. 1 (March 1952), pp. 77–91; Harry M. Markowitz, *Portfolio Selection: Efficient Diversification of Investments*, Cowles Foundation Monograph No. 16, (New York: John Wiley & Sons, 1959); William Sharpe, "A Simplified Model for Portfolio Analysis," *Management Science*, vol. 9, no. 2, (January 1963), pp. 277–293.

2.1 Characteristics of an Exposed Asset or Liability

It is assumed that the single most important factor affecting the return on exposed assets, or the cost of exposed liabilities is a devaluation.[2] This is expressed mathematically. First in the case of assets, define:

R_i = return on Asset i in constant dollars.

A_i = expected yield on asset in local currency without a devaluation.

$\tilde{C}_i$ = random variable with a mean of zero and a variance V_i (expresses nondevaluation uncertainties).

B_i = proportion of Asset i vulnerable to a devaluation.

$\tilde{d}$ = random variable = 0 if a devaluation does not occur.

      = 1 if a devaluation occurs.

$P = P(\tilde{d} = 1)$ = probability of a devaluation.

D = devaluation amount.

W = expected devaluation amount.

$\tilde{C}_D$ = random variable with a mean of zero and a variance V_D (expresses uncertainty as to the devaluation amount).

N = number of asset and liability variables.

Return on Asset i can be expressed as

$$R_i = A_i + \tilde{C}_i + B_i \tilde{d} D,$$

where the devaluation amount $D = W + \tilde{C}_D$. Therefore,

$$R_i = A_i + \tilde{C}_i + B_i \tilde{d}(W + \tilde{C}_D).$$

What does this equation mean? If there is no devaluation, that is, if $\tilde{d} = 0$, the last term disappears; in this case,

$$R_i = A_i + \tilde{C}_i.$$

The random variable $\tilde{C}_i$ expresses the uncertainty resulting from all factors other than devaluation. Its variance V_i measures the business risk.

When a devaluation occurs ($\tilde{d} = 1$), the return will be suddenly changed by the term $B_i \tilde{d}(W + \tilde{C}_D)$. In the case of an exposed asset, the return is reduced ($B_i < 0$). Therefore, a devaluation affects the return proportionately to the asset's vulnerability to the devaluation B_i and also proportionately to the mean amount of the devaluation W. In addition, a new source of uncertainty is introduced by the random variable $\tilde{C}_D$, expressing the uncertainty about the exact amount of the devaluation.

2. It is assumed, throughout this book, that a devaluation of "local currency" is in terms of the dollar. Revaluations can be treated similarly, simply by changing the sign of the W coefficients. (See Section 9.1.)

To express these assumptions graphically, a devaluation probability profile must be defined. Suppose that there is an 80% probability that a devaluation will not occur, and that, if it does occur, its most likely value would be 30%. Because this latter figure is not completely certain, suppose that a normal distribution with the mean value of 30% and a variance V_D better reflects reality (Figure 2.1). Also, suppose that

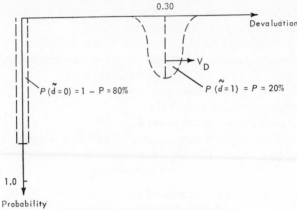

FIGURE 2.1   Devaluation Profile

the single period model has a time horizon short enough to have a constant devaluation probability profile. Given this devaluation profile, the assumptions on return of Asset i can be expressed on a graph (see Figure 2.2).

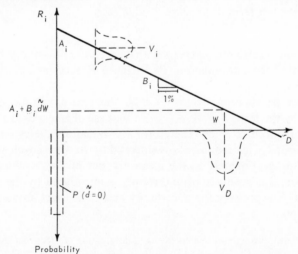

FIGURE 2.2   Effect of a Devaluation on an Exposed Asset

Without devaluation ($\tilde{d} = 0$), it is clear that the most likely value is A_i, but deviation from this value can occur owing to V_i. If a devaluation of magnitude W occurs, the return is reduced to $A_i + B_i \tilde{d}W$ where B_i is negative. Since W is not known with certainty either, a new source of uncertainty is introduced. The combined effect of V_i and V_D can put the actual return of Asset i anywhere in the shaded area of Figure 2.3 with a given probability.

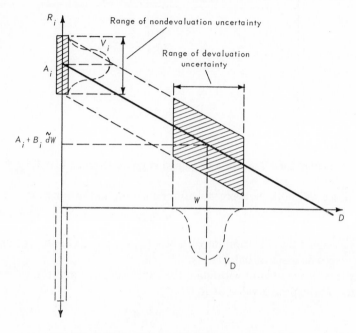

FIGURE 2.3   Effect of Uncertainties on an Exposed Asset

How would our assumptions change if we had an exposed liability, in local currency, instead of an asset? In the case of an exposed asset, there normally is a positive expected return ($A_i > 0$) and a negative vulnerability coefficient ($B_i < 0$). For a liability, the only difference will be the sign of those coefficients (that is, $A_i < 0$ and $B_i > 0$). Normally, a liability has a cost, and this cost, expressed in constant dollars, is reduced by a devaluation (see Figure 2.4).

In summary, the coefficient B_i can take all values between $+1$ and -1. An unexposed asset or liability, which is a variable whose return or cost is not affected by a devaluation, will be characterized by $B_i = 0$. From this point in the discussion, returns on assets and costs of

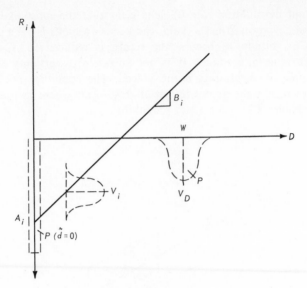

FIGURE 2.4   Effect of a Devaluation on an Exposed Liability

liabilities will both be expressed simultaneously in the equation

$$R_i = A_i + \tilde{C}_i + B_i \tilde{d}(W + \tilde{C}_D).$$

It is assumed that the random variables $\tilde{C}_i$, $\tilde{d}_i$, and $\tilde{C}_D$ are independent for a specific asset or liability.

It is now possible to formulate the expected value and the variance of R_i. The expected value of R_i is

$$E_i = A_i + B_i A_{N+1},$$

where

$$A_{N+1} = \text{expected value of } \tilde{d}(W + \tilde{C}_D)$$
$$= E(\tilde{d})W + E(\tilde{d})E(\tilde{C}_D)$$
$$= PW,$$

because the expected value of $\tilde{d}$ is the probability of a devaluation P, and $E(\tilde{C}_D) = 0$. The variance of R_i is

$$V_i' = V_i + B_i^2 V_{N+1}$$

where

$$V_{N+1} = \text{variance of } \tilde{d}(W + \tilde{C}_D)$$
$$= E[\tilde{d}^2(W + C_D)^2] - [E(\tilde{d})E(W + \tilde{C}_D)]^2$$
$$= E(\tilde{d}^2)E(W + \tilde{C}_D)^2 - [E(\tilde{d})E(W + \tilde{C}_D)]^2.$$

Since,

$$E(\tilde{d}) = P,$$
$$E(\tilde{d}^2) = P,$$
$$E(W + \tilde{C}_D) = W,$$
$$E(W + \tilde{C}_D)^2 = W^2 + V_D,$$

we have[3]

$$V_{N+1} = P(W^2 + V_D) - P^2 W^2$$
$$V_{N+1} = P[W^2(1 - P) + V_D].$$

The expected value E_i and variance V'_i of each asset or liability are composed of two parts: the direct contribution without devaluation effect (A_i and V_i) and the impact of a devaluation (the second terms).

The value of A_{N+1} will be referred to as a *devaluation coefficient*. It is simply the product of the devaluation probability and the mean of the devaluation amount. The variance of the devaluation coefficient is V_{N+1}. It reflects the contribution of the devaluation uncertainty to the variance of R_i.

2.2 Combinations of Assets and Liabilities

It was stated earlier that the treasurer is faced with a complex portfolio of assets and liabilities. It is possible now to compute the expected value and the variance of such a portfolio. A *portfolio* is a linear combination of these assets and liabilities.

The return of the full portfolio of hedging strategy is

$$R = \sum_{i=1}^{N} X_i R_i$$
$$= \sum_{i=1}^{N} X_i [A_i + \tilde{C}_i + B_i \tilde{d}(W + \tilde{C}_D)]$$
$$= \sum_{i=1}^{N} X_i (A_i + \tilde{C}_i) + \sum_{i=1}^{N} X_i B_i \tilde{d}(W + \tilde{C}_D),$$

where X_i is the amount of asset or liability i included in the portfolio and N is the total number of assets and liabilities in the period. Let

$$X_{N+1} = - \sum_{i=1}^{N} X_i B_i.$$

3. If a devaluation is certain ($P=1$) but its amount unknown, then $V_{N+1} = V_D$, measuring simply the uncertainty of the amount. Similarly, if a devaluation is not going to occur ($P = 0$), then $V_{N+1} = 0$, which means no devaluation risk at all. These results are what one should intuitively expect.

The physical meaning of X_{N+1} is "net exposure" or "net exposed assets;" that is, X_{N+1} is the total exposed assets minus the total exposed liabilities. The X_{N+1} represents the net amount that is vulnerable to devaluation losses.[4]

The return of the portfolio can be written as

$$R = \sum_{i=1}^{N} X_i (A_i + \tilde{C}_i) + X_{N+1} \, \tilde{d}(W + \tilde{C}_D).$$

In this equation, $\tilde{d}$ and $\tilde{C}_D$ are still independent random variables, but the $\tilde{C}_i$ of the different assets or liabilities are not necessarily independent of each other.

The uncertain costs of 2 future bank loans in the same period, or their business risk, are very likely to be positively correlated. Money market conditions will make these costs rise or fall together. The $\tilde{C}_i$ of these 2 loans will have a positive correlation coefficient, and this will increase the total variance of the strategy of that period.

The expected value E of the strategy's return is

$$E = \sum_{i=1}^{N} X_i A_i + X_{N+1} A_{N+1},$$

and the variance of the strategy's return is

$$V = \sum_{i=1}^{N} X_i^2 V_i + X_{N+1}^2 V_{N+1} + \sum_{i=1}^{N} \sum_{j=1}^{N} X_i X_j \, \text{cov} \, (\tilde{C}_i \tilde{C}_j),$$

where $i \neq j$.

The expected value of the portfolio or hedging strategy is made up of 2 components: (1) the direct contribution of each asset or liability to the total expected return or expected cost, and (2) the term reflecting the impact of a devaluation on this expected value. Analogously, the variance contains a term that reflects the direct contribution of each asset or liability to the total variance and another term that represents the impact of a devaluation on this variance. A third term takes into account the increased risk as a result of the correlation of business risks of different variables. These values can be rewritten as[5]

$$E = \sum_{i=1}^{N+1} X_i A_i,$$

$$V = \sum_{i=1}^{N+1} X_i^2 V_i + \sum_{i=1}^{N} \sum_{j=1}^{N} X_i X_j \, \text{cov} \, (\tilde{C}_i \tilde{C}_j),$$

4. In Sharpe's terms, it is the "investment in the index."
5. The reasons for the $N+1$ notation for the devaluation characteristics now become apparent. It was borrowed from: Kalman J. Cohen and Jerry A. Pogue, "An Empirical Evaluation of Alternative Portfolio Selection Models," *The Journal of Business of the University of Chicago* vol. 40, no. 2, (April 1967), pp. 166–193.

where $i \neq j$. The optimal selections of assets and liabilities are determined by the problem

$$\text{maximize } Z = LE - V,$$

where

$$L = \text{parameter varying from 0 to } \infty,$$

$$E = \sum_{i=1}^{N+1} X_i A_i,$$

$$V = \sum_{i=1}^{N+1} X_i^2 V_i + \sum_{i=1}^{N} \sum_{j=1}^{N} X_i X_j \operatorname{cov}(\tilde{C}_i \tilde{C}_j),$$

where $i \neq j$ and subject to

$$X_i \geq 0, \qquad i = 1, \ldots, N$$

$$X_{N+1} = \sum_{i=1}^{N} X_i B_i.$$

The preceding approach to the unitemporal model is actually a combination of the models of Markowitz and Sharpe for portfolio selection. Markowitz's covariance model contributes the correlation technique for the business risks; Sharpe's index model is used extensively with the adaptation of another type of index. Sharpe's "market index" becomes our devaluation amount $\tilde{d}D$. The correlation of 2 variables is accomplished directly (Markowitz's covariance technique) and indirectly through their common relationship with $\tilde{d}D$ (Sharpe's index technique).

The total correlation system in the unitemporal model can therefore be expressed graphically (see Figure 2.5). For instance, Asset i is

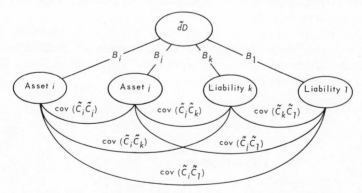

FIGURE 2.5   Correlation System of the Unitemporal Model

related to Liability k by 2 means. The cov $(\tilde{C}_i\tilde{C}_k)$ captures the direct correlation between these 2 variables, and simultaneously both are influenced by a common element $\tilde{d}D$.

2.3 Examples

Some simplified examples are included to explain the major characteristics of the unitemporal model.

2.3.1 Example: Two Assets

The problem is to allocate $1,000 to two different assets:

Asset 1: Investment yielding a return of 20% expressed in local currency. This return has a variance V_1. The variance reflects the fact that the absolute minimum on the return is at 14% and its maximum at 26%. This range is fairly large; that is, this asset has a relatively high business risk.

Asset 2: Investment yielding 15% when expressed in local currency but only exposed at 50% to a devaluation. The business risk is relatively smaller (range 12% to 18%). An interesting feature of this asset is that it is perfectly negatively correlated with the previous one. The negative correlation measures the tendency of the returns of these 2 assets to move in opposite directions: when Asset 1 has a higher return than expected (for example, 16%), Asset 2 will be lower than expected (for example, 12%), and vice versa. For example, these investments are in 2 products competing for the same market. If one does well, the other is likely to be in trouble.

The devaluation probability is estimated at 20%. The amount of the devaluation will be between 10% and 30%, with the most likely value at 20%. From these 3 values — the most likely amount, the absolute maximum, and the absolute minimum — the expected value and the variance are computed.

No speculation on currency depreciation is allowed. Therefore, the net exposure cannot be negative. The characteristics of the 2 assets and the devaluation profile are represented graphically in Figure 2.6. The coefficients for this problem are

$$
\begin{array}{ll}
A_1 = 0.2 & B_1 = -1 \\
A_2 = 0.15 & B_2 = -0.5 \\
V_1 = 0.004 & P = 0.2 \\
\dot{V}_2 = 0.0001 & W = 0.2 \\
\text{cov}\,(\tilde{C}_i\,\tilde{C}_j) = -0.0002 & V_{N+1} = 0.01 \\
& A_{N+1} = PW = 0.04
\end{array}
$$

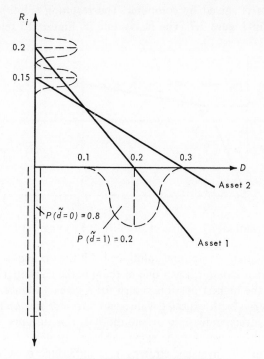

FIGURE 2.6   Input to Example 2.3.1

The expected values and variances of all the possible strategies with these 2 assets are

$$E = A_1 X_1 + A_2 X_2 + A_{N+1} X_{N+1},$$
$$V = V_1 X_1^2 + V_2 X_2^2 + V_{N+1} X_{N+1}^2 - X_1 X_2 \operatorname{cov} (\tilde{C}_i \tilde{C}_j),$$

and optimal solutions are determined by

$$\text{maximize } LE - V,$$

subject to

$X_{N+1} = X_1 + 0.5 X_2$	net exposure,
$X_1 + X_2 \leq 1000$	budget constraint,
$X_1 \geq 0$	no negative amounts can be purchased,
$X_2 \geq 0$	no negative amounts can be purchased,
$X_{N+1} \geq 0$	no speculation.

The problem is solved by computer. The resulting solution is shown graphically in Figure 2.7. The heavy line in Figure 2.7 represents the

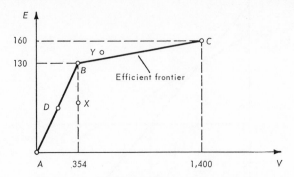

FIGURE 2.7   Efficient Frontier of Example 2.3.1

"efficient frontier" of optimal solutions.[6] All the optimal solutions are on this efficient frontier. Each one of them is the combination of both assets, with the highest possible return for a given variance.

The strategies with expected value and variance not on the efficient frontier are either unfeasible or suboptimal. For instance, strategy X is suboptimal because, for the same variance, strategy B has a higher expected return. Conversely, strategy Y is unfeasible because no combination of Asset 1 and Asset 2 will yield such a high return for the corresponding variance without violating one of the constraints (for instance, the budget constraint or the prohibition of speculation). The optimal strategies are determined by the parametric quadratic computer program. This program increases the values of the parameter L automatically in order to compute the successive strategies — the higher the value of the parameter, the greater the emphasis on expected cost reductions (or expected return increases). The values of the variables in each of the optimal strategies are represented in Figure 2.8.

Figure 2.8 is constructed as follows: The horizontal axis fundamentally represents variance, with the 3 optimal strategies selected for comment plotted along the axis at the variances that correspond to them. However, in order to avoid clutter, the actual distance AB has been made equal to BC, so that the scale of variances in the segment AB is larger than that in the segment BC, though it is linear within each segment. The vertical axis represents amounts in dollars, whether of cash, exposure, or assets. On this set of coordinates the 4 variables cash,

6. The term "efficient frontier" was coined by Markowitz in his portfolio theory work.

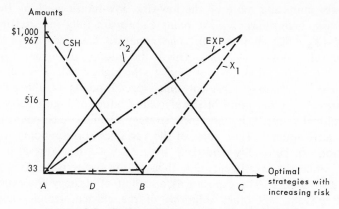

FIGURE 2.8   Optimal Strategies for Example 2.3.1

exposure X_1, and X_2 — as calculated for all the strategies on the efficient frontier — have each been plotted against the variance. Each point on the variance axis represents both a variance and the optimal strategy corresponding to it. If a vertical line is drawn through any point of the variance axis, the intersections of the line with the 4 curves give, for the optimal strategy corresponding to the particular variance, the amounts of cash, exposure, Asset 1, and Asset 2.

The first optimal solution, that of the extreme risk avoider, is strategy A: keep everything in cash (CSH = \$1,000; $X_1 = 0$; $X_2 = 0$ — where CSH represents the "investment" in cash, X_1 the amount invested in Asset 1, and X_2 the amount invested in Asset 2).[7] The expected return and risk are clearly zero, as can be read from Figure 2.7.

The second optimal solution, at B, is a low-risk strategy. Most of the investment is in the low-risk, low-return asset ($X_2 = \$967$). A small amount of the other asset is also purchased ($X_1 = \$33$) because of the negative correlation of the business risks. It reduces the overall risk to have some of each asset. If the return on Asset 2 is worse than we expect, we know that the other asset will do better than expected, and offset part of the losses. The exposure is already fairly high (EXP = \$516.5). The expected value of this strategy is \$130, with a variance[8] of 354.

As we move from strategy B to the next solution, strategy C, the model

7. Cash is in dollars, and therefore not exposed. The investments in the assets are in "local currency."
8. Section 1.4.1 allows one to translate this variance into intuitively meaningful data. For instance, if we assume a normal distribution, there is only a probability of less than 1/200 that the return on this strategy is worse than \$84.

replaces more and more of the low-risk, low-return asset X_2 by the high-risk, high-return X_1. At point C, we are fully invested in the latter ($X_2 = \$0$; $X_1 = \$1000$). The exposure has risen accordingly to the full exposure of \$1000. This is the solution of highest possible return ($E = 160$); it also corresponds to the highest risk ($V = 1400$).

These 3 solutions represent only special points of the efficient frontier. Any other point of the efficient frontier of Figure 2.7 is also an optimal solution. For instance, strategy D, midway between A and B, is also optimal. The values of the variables corresponding to this solution can be readily read from Figure 2.8. Cash is kept at a \$500 level, while the investments in both assets are respectively, $X_1 = \$16.5$ and $X_2 = \$483.5$. The exposure is also half of strategy B's exposure (EXP = \$258). All other solutions of the efficient frontier can be determined similarly by interpolation on the graphs of Figures 2.7 and 2.8.

The general tendency in the solutions of this problem is straightforward. From the complete risk-avoider solution (do nothing), one first moves into heavy investments in the low-risk asset. If the investor is bolder, he can invest instead in the high-risk asset up to the complete investment of all cash in that asset.

2.3.2 Four Assets, Three Liabilities, All Risks

The foregoing Example 2.3.1 was set up in a fashion such that intuitive solutions to it could be found. Since the number of variables was so small, no mathematical model was necessary to yield the results. The present example, although it is still insignificantly complicated in comparison with real-life devaluation hedging, does not permit such intuitive solutions. A little more confidence is required.

The first 2 available assets (X_1 and X_2) are identical to the corresponding variables of the previous example. The only difference is that now the business risks are assumed to be positively correlated; that is, when Asset 1 has a higher return than expected, so will Asset 2. The other variables are

Asset 3: Expected return and business risk fall between the characteristics of the two first assets: yield of 18% and a spread between 22.25% and 13.75%. This investment opportunity is completely exposed to a devaluation like Asset 1. Furthermore, it is perfectly negatively correlated to this latter asset.

Asset 4: Is a very low yielding asset (10%) in dollars. It is not exposed, and its return is known with certainty. It could represent,for example, a treasury bond in the United States and is completely independent of all the other investment opportunities previously referred to.

Liability 1: This variable represents a local bank loan with a most likely interest rate of 12%. The negotiations have not been concluded yet, and therefore the cost is still uncertain (range between 9% and 15%). The maximum amount of this loan is the equivalent of $5,000. As the loan is repayable in local currency, this is an exposed liability.

Liability 2: This loan is a bank loan raised in the United States. It is not exposed and has a low cost (6%). The uncertainty about this cost is also comparatively low (3% to 9%). The maximum available is $6,000.

Liability 3: A fairly expensive and uncertain loan (expected cost 16% and a spread between 11.75% and 20.25%). This exposed bank loan is available at the same local institution as Liability 1. It is therefore assumed that the costs of these 2 bank loans are perfectly positively correlated. The maximum available is $10,000.

Instead of there being $1,000 in cash available for investment as in Example 2.3.1, a working capital of $2,000 is required in the present problem.

The correlation system of this problem (the particular case of the general scheme represented in Figure 2.5) is shown in Figure 2.9.

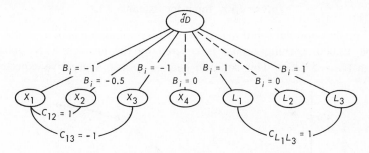

FIGURE 2.9   Correlation System for Example 2.3.2

All exposed variables are related to one another by their common relationship with $\tilde{d}D$. Some variables have also a business-risk covariance: X_1 and X_2 are positively correlated, as are L_1 and L_3. In contrast, X_1 and X_3 are negatively correlated.

The characteristics of the 7 variables are displayed in Figure 2.10. The slopes of the unexposed variables (Asset 4 and Liability 2) are zero. The devaluation outlook is the same as in the previous Example 2.3.1.

The efficient frontier and the values of the variables in each optimal strategy are found in Figure 2.11 and Table 2.1. A table is used because the graphs become cluttered when so many variables are in question. (It is useful to compare Figure 2.11 and Table 2.1 in reading text.)

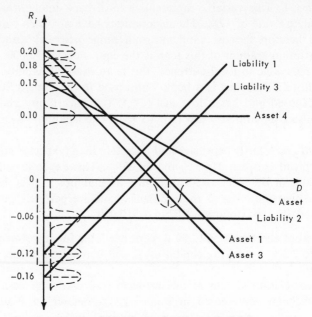

FIGURE 2.10   Input for Example 2.3.2

The first optimal solution (Strategy A) is a minimum action solution. The $2,000 working capital is covered by the low-cost U.S. dollar loan ($L_2 = \$2,000$). This solution has, of course, a negative expected

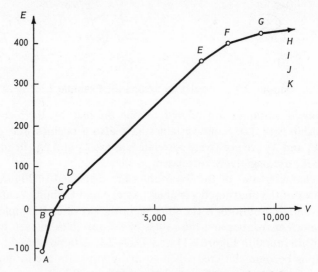

FIGURE 2.11   Efficient Frontier of Example 2.3.2

TABLE 2.1 Optimal Strategy for Example 2.3.2

Variables					Strategies						
	A	B	C	D	E	F	G	H	I	J	K
X_1		$592	$859	$948	$2,201	$2,255	$2,539	$4,882	$10,074	$10,326	$19,000
X_2				$161	$373	$500	$1,172	$3,121	$8,510	$8,673	
X_3		$744	$1,085	$1,231	$2,858	$2,844	$2,771	$4,711			
X_4					$2,642	$3,401	$2,518				
L_1		$1,336	$1,870	$2,154	$5,000	$5,000	$5,000	$5,000	$5,000	$5,000	$5,000
L_2	$2,000	$2,074	$2,186	$5,074	$6,000	$6,000	$6,000	$6,000	$6,000	$6,000	$6,000
L_3								$3,714	$9,584	$10,000	$10,000
EXP			$74	$106	$246	$349	$896	$2,439	$4,000	$4,000	$4,000
E^*	$-120	$-28	$15	$41	$360	$404	$438	$640	$893	$906	$1,080
V^*	400	705	1,053	1,320	7,112	8,315	9,766	28,917	78,082	81,541	193,518

* From Figure 2.11.

return. The risk is small but not zero because of the uncertainty about the exact cost of this loan.

The strategy represented by point B purchases some of the 2 negatively correlated assets and finances this purchase by raising exactly the amount of a local loan necessary to cover both investments (X_1 = \$592, X_2 = \$744, L_1 = \$1,336, L_2 = \$2,074). This operation allows almost a break-even result.

A similar strategy is applied in C, but a very small exposure is allowed (EXP = \$74), and the expected return becomes positive for the first time. A small net exposure seems to be required to break even in this problem.

Strategies D and E introduce, respectively, the purchase of new assets X_2 and X_4. The cheaper bank loans are now used at their maximum.

In the next 2 strategies (F and G), no new financing is used. A redistribution of the 4 assets yields a portfolio with a higher expected return, at an increased risk.

The expensive and uncertain loan L_3 is tapped for the first time in Strategy H. The cost of this loan is much larger than the return on the unexposed low-risk, low-yield asset X_4. This latter investment X_4 disappears from the portfolio, increasing drastically the net exposure (EXP = 2,439).

As more and more financing is done with the expensive loan, the portfolio concentrates on the higher yielding asset (X_1 = 10,074). The exposure becomes very large, the asset that is only exposed at 50% becomes more valuable (X_2 = 8,510) in strategy I.

In point J, this strategy is pushed up to the limit of all the available credit.

Finally, strategy K represents the investment of all available capital in the highest yielding asset. The strategy risk is now extremely high.

2.4 Selection of the Optimal Strategy

In each of the examples, an infinite set of optimal solutions has been given. The corner points have usually been described in more detail. But all the intermediate solutions can be readily deduced from the output data. The problem to tackle now is how to choose among all these optimal strategies. Clearly, the complete risk avoider and the extreme gambler have their solutions already determined: the extreme points at either end of the efficient frontier. But what solution is relevant for the more "normal" treasurer?

Classical utility theory is the most satisfying method. Utility theory is an extremely old concept; Daniel Bernouilli laid the groundwork for it in 1738.[9] Classical utility theory has been developed and used extensively in economics.[10] The reader is referred to the literature for a formal explanation of the theory. More recently, this concept has been used for investment decisions under uncertainty.[11]

In the version of expected return versus variance, utility preferences can be represented graphically (see Figure 2.12). The U_i curves repre-

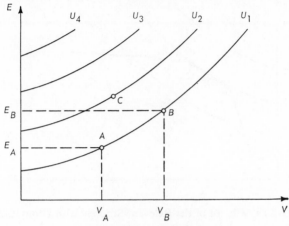

FIGURE 2.12   Utility Curves

sent utility curves for a specific investor. Each curve is the locus of those combinations of expected returns and variances that have the same utility. An investor is indifferent between A and B, because they are both on the same utility curve U_1. In other words, for this specific investor, the higher risk in $B(V_B > V_A)$ is perfectly offset by the increase in expected return $(E_B > E_A)$. The investment opportunity C is preferred to both A and B: It is on a higher utility curve.

Techniques, usually based on choices between lotteries, have been developed to derive the utility functions of individuals; applications to businessmen's risk aversion followed.[12] The use of this theory to select

9. "Specimen Theoriae Novae de Mensura Sortis," *Papers of the Imperial Academy of Sciences in Petersburg* vol. V, (1738), pp. 175–192.
10. Milton Friedman and Leonard Savage, "The Utility Theory of Choices Involving Risk," *The Journal of Political Economy* vol. LVI, no. 4 (August 1948), pp. 279–304.
11. J. Hirshleifer, "Investment Decisions under Uncertainty: Choice-Theoretic Approaches," *The Quarterly Journal of Economics* vol. LXXIX, no. 4, (November 1965), pp. 505–536.
12. Paul E. Green, "The Derivation of Utility Functions in a Large Industrial Firm," paper given at the First Joint National Meeting of the Operations Research Society of America and The Institute of Management Sciences, 1961; F. Mosteller and P. Nogel, "An Experimental Measurement of Utility," *Journal of Political Economy* vol. 59, no. 5, (1951), pp. 376–404.

the optimal strategy that best fits the preferences of a specific manager is simple (see Figure 2.13). Once the efficient frontier $ABCD$ has been determined, as in Examples 2.3.1 and 2.3.2, the utility curves are superimposed on this graph (Figure 2.13). The strategy on the highest possible

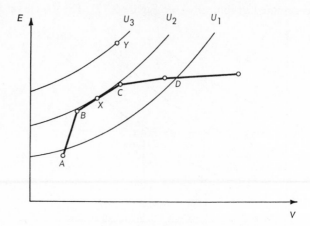

FIGURE 2.13   Choice of the Relevant Strategy with Utility Curves

utility curve is the optimal one for this specific case (point X on utility curve U_2). Strategy D, for example, is inferior, because it is on a lower utility curve. On the other hand, a strategy such as Y, on a still higher utility level, is unfeasible. The point of tangency of the highest possible utility curve automatically determines the best choice available. If this optimal strategy is not a corner point (like B or C), the exact values of all the variables are derived as in Example 2.3.1.

The method of deriving utility functions of individuals is the only theoretically satisfactory one. However, problems arise when the choice has to be made with the utility curves of a firm rather than of an individual. Whose utility curves should be used: the president's, the treasurer's, the stockholder's? This problem can become serious because utility theory has not been established to deal with the preferences of a large number of people at the same time, as for example the stockholders of a company.

In an operational devaluation-hedging model, some rough guidelines can be set. One way is simply to determine the maximum amount the company is willing to lose in a specific country with a given probability: for example, \$50,000 with a probability of less than 1/100. The variance is computed for this strategy, and the optimal strategy can be determined graphically (point X in Figure 2.14).

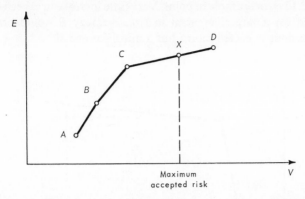

FIGURE 2.14   Choice of the Relevant Strategy with a Maximum-Risk
Criterion

Another simplification of utility theory that could be operationally
useful is the determination of a marginal expected return versus
variance criterion. This concept could be more precise than the previous
technique. For example, the maximum-accepted-risk criterion determines the optimal strategy X in Figure 2.15. It could be that manage-

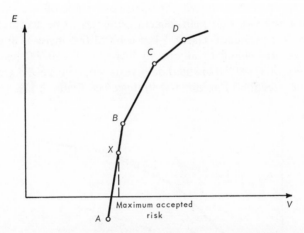

FIGURE 2.15   Example of Difficulty Resulting from Maximum-Risk Criterion

ment would be willing to relax its maximum-accepted-risk constraint,
in view of the sizable increments of expected return, for a low increase
in accepted risk.

In other cases, it could be of interest to reduce the accepted-risk level.

Figure 2.16 is an example in point. Very little increase in expected return is gained for a large increment in risk. Strategy B would practically have the same expected return but a much lower risk.

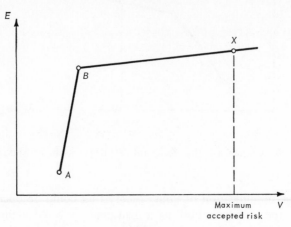

FIGURE 2.16   Another Example of Difficulty Resulting from Maximum-Risk Criterion

The marginal expected return versus variance criterion would alleviate this problem by giving the particular trade-off between expected return and risk that management estimates to be acceptable. For example, management declares, "For each $1,000 increase in expected return, we are willing to accept an increase of $50,000 loss with a probability of 1/100." This method gives a slope in the EV graph that allows the selection of an optimal strategy (see Figure 2.17).

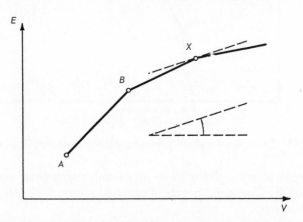

FIGURE 2.17   Marginal Expected-Return-versus-Variance Criterion

On purely theoretical grounds, these 2 shortcuts are not valid. The model, as we noted in Section 1.4.2, assumes quadratic utility functions as in Figure 2.13. However, for operational use, these shortcuts are appealing because of their simplicity.

The unitemporal model is the basic building block of the devaluation-hedging model. As explained in the next chapter by relating a set of such blocks to one another, the full multitemporal model is developed.

3
The Multitemporal Model

3.1 The Model

Why is a multitemporal model needed? Timing in devaluation hedging is extremely critical. The decisions made now can affect the exposure and, hence, the devaluation risk many months in the future. The problem is complicated by the imperfections and fluctuations of the capital markets in devaluation-prone currencies. When a devaluation is close, short-term credit and forward-exchange contracts can simply disappear from the market or become very expensive. Therefore, hedging has to be planned for a reasonably long period of time in the future.

Another important reason for developing a multitemporal model is that optimizing each period independently does not guarantee even good, let alone optimal solutions in the total time horizon. For example, the optimal decision in the first month could be to neglect forward-exchange contracts. Six months later, if a devaluation is likely and no futures are available, optimal over-all strategy might contradict the first month's optimal solution. Having the forward-exchange contracts available at the critical moment might justify carrying their costs during the previous periods. An optimal strategy is not a succession of independent optimal decisions but the best set of decisions over the whole time horizon. Therefore, a multitemporal model is essential in devaluation hedging.

How is the model made multitemporal? Two means will be used simultaneously. The first method is simply to include a large number of constraints covering different periods. The same variable appearing in different time-period constraints increases the interweaving of the unitemporal models into a single multitemporal model. Orgler,[1] for

1. Yair Orgler, "An Unequal-Period Model for Cash Management By Business Firms," Federal Deposit Insurance Corporation. Paper presented at the TIMS/ORSA Joint Meeting, San Francisco, Calif. May 1968.

example, in his multitemporal model for cash management, does exactly that. The second technique, and the more powerful one — to bind tightly together the successive time periods — is new. To understand it, the notion of covariance of risk over time must be introduced.

Risk is measured by a variance in this model. The total variance of a strategy is not simply equal to the sum of the variances of the unitemporal models. The covariance of the returns in the different time periods must be added. If R_1 is the return on a strategy in the first period and R_2 the return on a strategy in the second period, then the total variance equals the variance R_1 plus the variance R_2 plus the covariance $R_1 R_2$. The last factor, covariance $R_1 R_2$, is binding the 2 unitemporal models tightly together.

In further analysis, the principle of Markowitz's covariance model for portfolio selection is used to intercorrelate the risks of successive periods. The following definitions are necessary:

L = parameter varying from 0 to ∞.

R_k = return on period k's decisions.

E_k = expected return on period k's decisions.

V_k = variance of period k's decisions.

C_{km} = devaluation covariance.

W_k = expected devaluation amount of period k.

D_k = devaluation amount of period k; where $(D_k = W_k + \tilde{C}_{Dk})$.

X_{ik} = amount of asset or liability i included in "portfolio" of period k.

A_{ik} = expected yield on asset or liability i without taking into account the devaluation in period k.

B_{ik} = proportion of asset or liability i vulnerable to a devaluation in period k.

A_{N+k} = devaluation coefficient of period k; (probability of a devaluation) $\times$ (expected amount of the devaluation) = $P_k W_k$.

V_{N+k} = variance of period k's devaluation coefficient.

X_{N+k} = net exposure in period k.

P_k = devaluation probability in period k.

$\tilde{d}_k$ = random variable = 0 if devaluation does not occur in period k;
                   = 1 if devaluation occurs in period k.

$\tilde{C}_{Dk}$ = random variable with zero mean, measuring uncertainty about devaluation amount of period k; its variance is V_{Dk}.

$\tilde{C}_{ik}$ = random variable with zero mean, measuring business risk of variable i in period k; its variance is V_{ik}.

N = number of assets and liabilities in the period.

T = number of periods.

In the Mathematical Appendix, it is proved that

$$\text{cov}\,(R_k R_m) = \sum_{i=1}^{N} \sum_{j=1}^{N} X_{ik} X_{jm} \,\text{cov}\,(\tilde{C}_{ik}\tilde{C}_{jm}) + X_{N+k} X_{N+m} C_{km},$$

where

$$C_{km} = W_k W_m \,\text{cov}\,(\tilde{d}_k \tilde{d}_m) + \text{cov}\,(\tilde{d}_k \tilde{d}_m)\,\text{cov}\,(\tilde{C}_{Dk}\tilde{C}_{Dm})$$
$$+ P_k P_m \,\text{cov}\,(\tilde{C}_{Dk}\tilde{C}_{Dm}),$$

where C_{km} is the devaluation covariance.

These equations, seemingly complicated, are in fact reflecting relatively simple notions. The first term

$$[\textstyle\sum_{i=1}^{N} \sum_{j=1}^{N} X_{ik} X_{jm} \,\text{cov}\,(\tilde{C}_{ik}\tilde{C}_{jm})]$$

refers to the fact that business risks can be correlated over time. In the unitemporal model, the costs of all bank loans tend to increase or decrease together, increasing the strategy risk of the period in question. The multitemporal model takes into account the similar tendency of costs to change in the same direction over time. The interest on long-term loans is an example of this behavior. If the interest cost this month is higher than last month's, next month's rate will tend to rise also. Adjustments on long-term credit are made gradually, and trends are observable. Therefore, if X_{ik} is a long-term loan in month k and X_{jm} a similar loan in month m, a positive correlation will probably exist between these 2 variables. The total variance of the strategy will be increased by $X_{ik} X_{jm} \,\text{cov}\,(\tilde{C}_{ik}\tilde{C}_{jm})$.

The second term $(X_{N+k} X_{N+m} C_{km})$ involves all the correlations of the devaluation characteristics: probabilities and amounts. When $\text{cov}\,(\tilde{d}_k \tilde{d}_m) > 0$, there is a tendency for devaluation probabilities to move in unison. Similarly, $\text{cov}\,(\tilde{C}_{Dk} \tilde{C}_{Dm}) > 0$ measures the tendency of the possible devaluation amounts to move up or down together.

In operational use, some of these covariances will be set to zero, a procedure that simplifies the data processing. In the present discussion, however, the concern is with all the possible relationships between variables. The general multitemporal model deals with the most general problem. It will be very easy to adapt it to realistic dimensions by simply neglecting some relationships if they are judged to be less critical.

The general multitemporal model is

$$\text{maximize } Z = L \sum_{k=1}^{T} E_k - \sum_{k=1}^{T} V_k - \sum_{k=1}^{T} \sum_{m=1}^{T} C_{km} X_{N+k} X_{N+m}$$
$$- \sum_{k=1}^{T} \sum_{m=1}^{T} \sum_{i=1}^{N} \sum_{j=1}^{N} X_{ik} X_{jm} \,\text{cov}\,(\tilde{C}_{ik}\tilde{C}_{jm}) \qquad (k \neq m, i \neq j)$$

where

$$E_k = \sum_{i=1}^{N} X_{ik} A_{ik} + X_{N+k} A_{N+k} \qquad k = 1, \ldots, T$$

$$V_k = \sum_{i=1}^{N} X_{ik}^2 V_{ik} + X_{N+k}^2 V_{N+k}$$

$$+ \sum_{i=1}^{N} \sum_{j=1}^{N} X_{ik} X_{jk} \operatorname{cov}(\tilde{C}_{ik} \tilde{C}_{jk}) \qquad k = 1, \ldots, T; \, i \neq j$$

subject to

$$X_{ik} \geq 0 \qquad \text{for all } i \text{ and all } k;$$

$$X_{N+k} = \sum_{i=1}^{N} X_{ik} B_{ik} \qquad k = 1, \ldots, T.$$

3.2 Examples

Some examples are included to explain the use of multitemporal models.

3.2.1 *Example: Two Periods, Five Assets, Four Liabilities*

This example is intended to demonstrate the importance of using multitemporal models in financing and devaluation hedging. Two periods are treated simultaneously. The first period is identical to that of Example 2.3.2. The same devaluation profile and the same available assets and liabilities as obtained there characterize the first of the periods now considered.

In the second period, the probability and the amount of the possible devaluation are much higher. A new high-yield asset and a fairly expensive loan are also made available during this period.

The variables are

X_{11} This asset is identical to X_1 of Example 2.3.2. (The first index number in the subscript refers to the period; the second is the number that identifies the asset itself within the given period — that is, this is asset 1, available in period 1.)

X_{12} is identical to X_2 of Example 2.3.2.
X_{13} „   „   „ X_3 „   „   „
X_{14} „   „   „ X_4 „   „   „
L_{11} „   „   „ L_1 „   „   „
L_{12} „   „   „ L_2 „   „   „
L_{13} „   „   „ L_3 „   „   „

X_{21} is the new high-yield exposed asset available in the second period. Its most likely return is 24%, with a spread between 21% and 27%.

L_{21} is a loan available at the same time. But the money market, in expectation of a devaluation, is tighter. The effective interest rate is anywhere between 9.8% and 18.2%, with the most likely cost at 14%. Only $3,000 can be raised at these conditions.

It is assumed that the transactions in the first period cannot be canceled in the second. For example, an asset purchased in the first period cannot be sold in the second.

The graph representing the assumptions relevant for the first period is Figure 2.10. The same data for the second period are given in Figure 3.1. The devaluation probability has risen to 80%, and its most likely

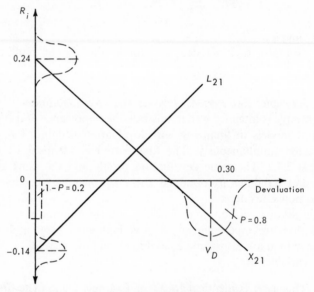

FIGURE 3.1   Variables of Period 2 in Problem 3.2.1

value is now 30%. The corresponding values in the first period were only 20% in both instances. One expects a much higher devaluation problem in the second period than in the first. The assumption about the correlations of devaluation amounts and probabilities is simply that they are perfectly positively correlated, that is, $\text{cov}(\tilde{C}_{D_1}, \tilde{C}_{D_2})$ $= \text{cov}(\tilde{d}_1, \tilde{d}_2) = 1$.

Figure 3.2 displays the efficient frontier for this problem, and Table 3.2 lists the values of each variable at each corner of the frontier.

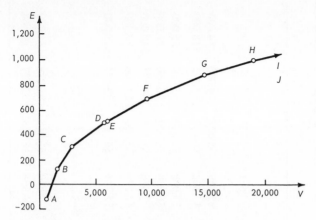

FIGURE 3.2 Efficient Frontier of Problem 3.2.1

The first optimal strategy A is the usual minimum action solution. It is the same as in Example 2.3.2: the $2,000 working capital requirements of the first period are covered by the low-cost dollar loan (L_{12} = $2,000). The very small risk in this strategy is paid by a negative expected return.

The impact of the second period on the unitemporal problem is revealed immediately in strategy B. The higher yield of the asset in the second period is very attractive. But as the loan available in the second period is expensive, the model suggests raising money in the first period with a low-cost local loan (L_{11} = $2,000), keeping it idle during the first period (CSH 1 = $2,000) and investing it immediately in the high-yield asset at the beginning of the second period (X_{21} = $2,000).

The exposure remains zero in both months, because the cash in the first month period and the exposed asset in the second are both covered by the same local loan. Referring to the unitemporal example (Table 2.1) it is obvious that this strategy is better than the one achieved by maximizing simply the first-period strategy. Comparatively, the multitemporal problem brings us out of the red at a relatively low-risk level.

Strategy C brings in the asset which is only exposed at 50% (X_{12} = $500). Half of the required financing comes from the cheaper unexposed loan (L_{12} = $2,250, of which $2,000 is used for the working capital requirement). More of the exposed loan is raised to cover and finance the high-yield asset in the second period.

The next 2 strategies D and E are very close to each other. The unexposed but low-yielding asset X_{14} is now part of the portfolio.

From Strategies F to J, the portfolio is increasingly dominated by the high-yielding asset X_{21}. The financing sources are tapped to the

TABLE 3.1 Optimal Strategies of Problem 3.2.1

	A	B	C	D	E	F	G	H	I	J
Variables										
X_{11}										
X_{12}			$500	$714	$691	$589	$661	$735		
X_{13}										
X_{14}				$857	$926	$2,408	$3,669	$3,632	$4,000	$4,000
X_{21}		$2,000	$3,250	$4,642	$4,654	$5,881	$7,322	$8,800	$12,475	$18,000
L_{11}	$2,000	$2,000	$3,500	$5,000	$5,000	$5,000	$5,000	$5,000	$5,000	$5,000
L_{12}		$2,000	$2,250	$3,214	$3,271	$4,703	$6,000	$6,000	$6,000	$6,000
L_{13}							$576	$1,167	$4,475	$10,000
L_{21}						$1,175	$2,076	$3,000	$3,000	$3,000
CSH 1		$2,000	$3,250	$4,642	$4,654	$4,705	$5,245	$5,800	$9,475	$15,000
CSH 2										
EXP 1										
EXP 2										
E^*	$-120	$119	$300	$514	$517	$693	$880	$1,018	$1,298	$1,739
V^*	400	1,119	2,812	5,739	5,784	9,310	14,304	18,908	32,737	69,464

* From Figure 2.1

maximum extent available. The expected return is increasing rapidly but the corresponding risk levels are also. Because of the very high devaluation coefficients and variances, all the optimal strategies require a zero net exposure.

This example has shown, by comparison with Example 2.3.2, how optimal solutions differ when one optimizes each period independently, or when a multitemporal model is used. It also demonstrates how the financing and hedging decisions are intimately related to each other. For example, the unexposed dollar loan L_{12} is used systematically to fill in cash requirements whenever it does not create a positive net exposure. Finally, the manipulation of internal cash flows to optimize the overall strategy is demonstrated in this simple case by the accumulation of cash from the first period to be invested in the second.

3.2.2. *Example: Four Periods, Forty-eight Variables*

The major purpose of this example is to acquaint the reader with a problem of a size between the very simplistic examples discussed up to now and the typically very large and complex problems the model is designed to handle. A "normal," real-life financing and hedging problem has several hundreds of variables and constraints. A somewhat simplified case study is presented in Chapter 4. It contains over 100 variables and over 150 constraints for a nine-period model.

In the present example, the focus is entirely on short-term financial management. No capital budgeting options are available. It is assumed that these decisions have already been made and that the treasurer simply wants to implement them at a minimum cost and risk. The problem is analyzed on a year time horizon, with quarterly data. There will be 4 periods in the model, each period representing one quarter. No attempts are made to make this example realistic in terms of the values of the coefficients used.

The treasurer's outlook for the devaluation profiles of each quarter is summarized in Table 3.2. From this data, the devaluation coefficients

TABLE 3.2   Devaluation Data

	Probability of a Devaluation	Most Likely Value of a Devaluation	Spread of Possible Devaluation Amounts
Quarter 1	0	—	—
Quarter 2	50%	15%	12%–18%
Quarter 3	10%	15%	9%–21%
Quarter 4	80%	20%	11%–29%

and the variances are computed. The correlations of the devaluation probabilities and amounts are again assumed to be equal to $+1$. All other correlations are neglected in this example. The cash budget the treasurer has to satisfy is simple:

Quarter 1: $2,000
Quarter 2: $3,000
Quarter 3: $10,000
Quarter 4: $4,000

In addition, the current operations result in a positive net exposure that the treasurer cannot avoid. Since some local loans run out in the next year, this exposure increases over time. His exposure budget or basic exposure (to be defined in Section 4.3.3) is as follows:

Quarter 1: $1,000
Quarter 2: $5,000
Quarter 3: $7,000
Quarter 4: $10,000

What are the options and decisions the treasurer can take to deal with these constraints? The first set of options are loans of different costs and maturities in each quarter:

L_{k1} (where k represents the quarter number) is the cheapest local loan available. Its most likely effective annual interest rate is 10%. The spread of the cost is between 7% and 13%. Interest and principal are payable at the maturity of 6 months. Only small amounts are available on these terms (see Table 3.3).

TABLE 3.3   Maximum Available Amounts of Local Loans

	Maximum on L_{k1}	Maximum on L_{k2}
Quarter 1	1,000	2,000
Quarter 2	500	1,000
Quarter 3	500	1,000
Quarter 4	500	1,500

L_{k2} is a similar loan, but with a higher expected annual cost (15%). The uncertainty about this cost is also slightly higher than for L_{k1}, but larger amounts are available (Table 3.3).

L_{k3} is the most expensive type of local loan available (20%). The maturity is also 2 quarters. At this price, there are no limits on the amounts one can borrow, but the uncertainty about the exact cost is fairly high.

L_{k4} are U.S. dollar loans at 6%. They are not exposed and they mature after one year. The uncertainty about this cost is typically small.

L_{25} in the second quarter, a special local loan with a one-year maturity, is available at a 12% interest cost. Only $2,000 could be borrowed at this price. The spread of the actual cost on this exposed liability is relatively narrow.

In addition to the loan decisions, the treasurer can purchase a limited amount of forward-exchange contracts. These contracts will be discussed in detail later (Section 4.7), but at this time it suffices to recall that they are a device to reduce the net exposure without changing the financing position. The "premium" or cost of these forward-exchange contracts is 0.5% per quarter. In the first 6 months, $3,000 in forward-exchange contracts are available per quarter, and only $2,000 per quarter are available during the balance of the year.

As an alternative to keeping idle cash, the treasurer can buy or sell treasury bonds with a given official yield of 6% per quarter. These treasury bonds are exposed assets. The only constraint is, of course, that no more treasury bonds can be sold in one period than have been accumulated from previous periods.

The example just described brings some new elements into the multitemporal model. The first is the problem of maturities. In all the previous examples, it was assumed implicitly that all the transactions had identical maturities, beyond the time horizon of the model. In the present case, the local loans L_{11}, L_{12}, and L_{13} mature in the third quarter. Therefore their repayment, interest, and principal, has to be budgeted for that time.

To help in the interpretation of the results, the costs and profits made by the decisions in each period will be accounted for separately, including the ones beyond the time horizon of the model. The costs and profits will be attributed to the quarter in which their cash outflow or inflow occurs. For example, the costs from the loan of the first period L_{11} will be recorded in the third quarter when the interest expenses are due. The costs on L_{31} or L_{41}, of the third and fourth quarter respectively, will be part of the costs incurred beyond the time horizon of the model, because they mature only then.

Another novelty in this example is the introduction of variables that are not really assets or liabilities but behave as if they were. The forward-exchange contract is not an asset or a liability, but its behavior is similar to that of an exposed liability.

The reduction of the net exposure is the one aspect a forward-exchange contract has in common with a local loan. The cost of that contract — its *premium* — is a cost only if the devaluation does not occur (Figure 3.3). If a devaluation of magnitude W materializes, a

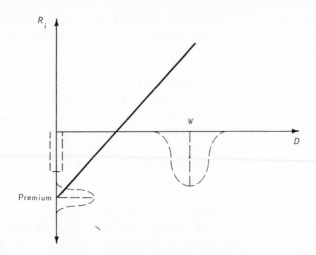

FIGURE 3.3   Effect of Devaluation on Forward-Exchange Contracts

devaluation profit can be made. Figure 3.3 is identical to Figure 2.4, where the behavior of an exposed liability was depicted. More is said about forward-exchange contracts in Section 4.7.

Only a few representative strategies of the solution are discussed here; the total number of optimal strategies are too large to handle. The representative strategies are shown in Table 3.4. For each strategy, the value of the parameter L, the expected cost E, and the variance V are given, as well as the values of all the variables. Only the nonzero variables are listed. Those listed are defined as follows:

XP $k1$ =(where k represents the quarter number) the purchases
            of treasury bonds in period k.

XS $k1$ =sales of treasury bonds in quarter k.

FEC k =the forward-exchange contracts purchased in quarter k.

CST k =the costs incurred in period k.

 CST* =the cost "beyond the time horizon" of the problem.

COST =simply the total costs of the strategy
          $(= \sum_{k=1}^{4} 1 \text{ CST } k + \text{CST*})$.

TABLE 3.4   Optimal Strategies of Problem 3.2.2

			Strategies		
	A	D	F	W	Z
L	0	5	50	300	∞
E	$1,463	$1,155	$684	$24	$706
V	7,439	7,911	18,126	87,843	450,682
XP 11		$2,418	$4,865	$19,562	$31,498
XP 21		$1,803	$1,547	$6,831	$14,724
XS 31		$4,221	$2,217	$12,562	$12,731
XS 41			$4,194	$10,331	$20,756
L 11	$78	$1,000	$1,000	$1,000	$1,000
L 12		$748	$2,000	$2,000	$2,000
L 13			$865	$7,588	$16,136
L 14	$1,922	$2,663	$3,000	$10,973	$14,361
L 21	$500	$500	$500	$500	$500
L 22	$921	$1,000	$1,000	$1,000	$1,000
L 23	$216	$133	$1,047	$6,331	$14,224
L 24	$1,622	$1,169			
L 25	$2,000	$2,000	$2,000	$2,000	$2,000
L 31	$500	$500	$500	$500	$500
L 32	$1,000	$1,000	$1,000	$1,000	$1,000
L 33	$1,861	$1,866	$2,550	$7,500	$16,734
L 34	$4,462	$4,271	$7,899		
L 41	$500	$500	$500	$500	$500
L 42	$1,500	$1,500	$1,443		
L 43	$1,590	$1,406			
L 44	$2,164	$2,340	$615	$1,743	
FEC 2	$704	$1,112	$3,000	$3,000	$3,000
FEC 3			$1,600	$2,000	$2,000
FEC 4	$1,048	$1,227	$2,000	$2,000	$2,000
EXP 1	$922	$1,669	$2,000	$9,973	$13,361
EXP 2	$2,840	$2,727		$7,973	$11,361
EXP 3			$931		$2,532
CSH 2	$2,261				
CST 3		$111	$301	$973	$1,828
CST 4	$115	$113	$212	$743	$1,532
CST*	$1,113	$1,124	$1,089	$1,506	$2,479
COST	$1,256	$1,343	$1,598	$3,226	$5,840
PRT 2		$145	$291		$1,883
PRT 3		$253	$384	$1,173	$2,773
PRT 4			$251	$1,583	$2,009
PRT*				$823	$764
PROF		$398	$928	$3,797	$7,936

PRT k = the profits on treasury bonds realized in period k.

PRT* = the profit "beyond the time horizon."

PROF = the total profit of the strategy ($= \sum_{k=1}^{4} = 1$ PRT k + PRT*).

CSH k = the cash on hand in period k.

When $L = 0$, the model is concerned only with minimizing the variance, without considering the expected return (Strategy A). The solution represents basically the minimum action: fulfill the cash requirements with the loans with low variance and reduce the net exposure if this is easy to do. For example, the $2,000 cash requirements of the first quarter are met by the low-risk dollar loan ($L_{14} = 1,922$) and some of the cheap and low-risk local loans ($L_{11} = 78$).

In the second quarter, more money is raised than is actually necessary to meet the cash requirements of that period and is accumulated in cash (CSH $2 = 2,261$) in order to supply the very large funds required in the third quarter. The $10,000 needed in this latter period stretches the cheapest loans available at that time to their maximum ($L_{31} = 500$ and $L_{32} = 1,000$). The balance comes from the more expensive local loan, the dollar loan, and the cash accumulated in the previous quarter.

The forward-exchange contracts are used only in the quarter in which the probability of a devaluation is highest. In the fourth quarter, this probability is considered high enough to cover completely the balance of the net exposure with forward-exchange contracts.

Finally, the costs of this strategy are substantial, especially beyond the time horizon (CST $4 = 115$ and CST* $= 1,113$). The total cost outlays are not far from realizing the expected costs (COST $= 1,256$ and $E = 1,465$). The discrepancy between E and the total cost outlays is because of the expected devaluation losses in the second quarter.

The second strategy (Strategy D) is not fundamentally different in regard to the financing decisions. The major difference results from the manipulation of treasury bonds as a financing source during periods when money is tight. The cheaper money available in the first quarter ($L_{11} = 1,000$ and $L_{12} = 748$) is used to purchase treasury bonds (XP $11 = 2,418$). In the second quarter, instead of accumulating idle cash, some more treasury bonds are purchased (XP $21 = 1,803$). All the short-term paper accumulated in this fashion is then sold in the third quarter (XS $31 = 4,221$) to help relieve the cash shortage at that time.

These operations result in a slightly higher total cost (COST $= 13,49$), but a profit is made on the bond transactions. Some bonds, held for 2 quarters, create a profit in the second and third quarters (quarterly dividend payments are assumed). To this profit, the dividends from the bonds held only for one quarter are added. (PRT $2 = 145$ and PRT $3 = 253$). Total bond profits are also computed (PROF $= 398$).

Strategy F is even more concerned with minimizing cost at the expense of an increase in risk ($E = 684$ and $V = 18,126$). All the cheaper local loans are now used at capacity, and even the more expensive ones are used extensively. Now bond transactions are made during all 4 quarters: purchases in the first two, sales in the last two. The forward-exchange contracts in the quarters in which the devaluation probability is high are now used at full capacity (FEC 2 = 3,000 and FEC 4 = 2,000). The net exposure is reduced to zero during these periods. This strategy results in higher interest expenses of another $250, but the profits from the treasury bonds more than offset this increase (they augment it by $530).

The next strategy W makes in fact more profit than the amount of the total interest expenses (PROF = 3,797 and COST = 3,226). But the exposure in the second quarter is fairly high and creates a substantial expected devaluation loss. This is why the total expected cost is still positive. As one would expect, this strategy involves very large bond transactions (XP 11 = 19,562 and XP 21 = 6,831), the bulk of which is sold in the third and fourth quarter, making XS 31 = 12,562 and XS 41 = 10,331). Notice that some of these bonds are not sold at all and produce a dividend inflow beyond the time horizon (PRT* = 829).

These transactions are financed by the loans on which no maximum constraints were put: the dollar loans and the most expensive local loans. The forward-exchange contracts are used at capacity. It is interesting to notice that none of the optimal strategies makes use of the forward-exchange contracts available in the first quarter. Because the probability of a devaluation in the first quarter is zero, no expenditure should be made to reduce the net exposure during that period.

The last strategy (Strategy Z) is the one corresponding to an unbounded value of the parameter L. Even if the expected devaluation loss is taken into account, the expected cost is negative. This strategy maximizes expected return without consideration of risk. The variance is therefore extremely high ($V = 450,682$). The bond transactions attain very high levels, with a total profit of $7,436. The use of the very expensive loans boosts the financing costs to $5,840. All financing and hedging is stretched to its maximum, especially in the first two quarters in which the purchases of treasury bonds are made.

Example 3.2.2, just discussed, shows how the model is expanded toward more realistic problems. There is nothing to prevent the handling of a still larger selection of financial and hedging transactions, during an expanded planning period. A case study approximating real-life data is presented in Chapter 4.

4

Adaptations to Specific International Financial Transactions: Ace International Corporation

The theoretical multitemporal model of Chapter 3 gives only the framework of the devaluation-hedging model; many more constraints exist in the international environment than those presented. Each situation requires some special constraints. To present a sample of such constraints, a case study of a mythical international corporation is presented: Ace International Corporation.

Section 4.1 presents a brief description of Ace International. The concern is with the financial relationship between the United States headquarters and its subsidiary in Brazil. The Brazilian devaluation outlook is the topic of Section 4.2. Section 4.3 presents the framework of the Ace International problem and gradually introduces the key variables and notations. Finally, a variety of international transactions relevant to hedging and/or financing are analyzed. The manner in which these transactions are incorporated into the model is also described in detail.

The Ace International case does not intend to represent a realistic situation, which would require a larger number of variables for each type of transaction. A large variety of types of variables are included, but only a few transactions of each type. It is fairly rare that all the types of operations presented here apply to any specific country at a given time. In the case of Brazil, during the historical period on which this case was built,[1] only local loans, straight dollar loans, and a few forward-exchange contracts were available, but almost 100 local loan variables were needed for a real problem. In this case study, only

1. Between November 1965, and February 1967. These dates have been chosen because a devaluation occurred within each of these two boundary months. This 16-month period allows a study from the day after a devaluation occurs to the next change in parity. These 16 months are condensed into 9 months to reduce the number of variables.

four kinds of bank loans are included, because the extension to a larger variety is fairly straightforward. On the other hand, we study financial and export swaps, different treasury bond operations, inventory hedgings, and repatriation of profits, in order to display how these transactions could be included in the model. (Chapter 8 is devoted to the actual implementation of the model on an operational basis.)

Two major limitations are imposed in this case study: the concern is with current financing only; and the optimizations made are exclusively pretax. In other words, capital budgeting is not explicitly considered, and tax implications are completely overlooked. These limitations will be dropped in the extensions of the basic model.[2]

The problem is simplified by assuming that all "business risks" are independent. No conceptual difficulties are involved in dropping this constraint. It allows the presentation of each type of financial or hedging transaction separately.

Finally, it is assumed that all transactions occur on the first day of the month in which they happen. This assumption could also be relaxed by taking very short periods in the model (for example, weeks or days).

4.1 Description of Ace International Corporation

Ace International is a diversified multinational company with headquarters in New York. Total sales are over one billion dollars, of which 65% are scattered in over 80 foreign countries around the world. Ace International has only 100%-owned subsidiaries. In addition to its worldwide marketing and distribution organization, it has 12 manufacturing companies outside the United States. Its products range from consumer products to industrial equipment, and a diversification move initiated in the late fifties is still increasing this product scope.

At this point, only the relationship of the headquarters with the operations in Brazil is considered. More specifically, only the protection of working capital against a devaluation of the cruzeiro is studied. Ace International has a manufacturing facility and a distribution chain in Brazil. Its main product lines in that country are vacuum cleaners and electrical appliances, both sold on an installment basis. These installment sales are the main cause of the large working capital needs of Ace International in Brazil. The planning horizon is short — nine months. During this period, the Brazilian subsidiary has a total requirement of about 39 billion cruzeiros (equivalent to 17 million dollars)

2. See Sections 7.2 and 6.3, respectively.

for new financing (mostly for its credit installment sales), and for repayment of loan contracts. Local loans, swaps, and straight dollar loans from the New York headquarters are available to satisfy these requirements. Under certain conditions, forward exchange can be purchased to reduce the exposure. Repatriation of profits is also possible at a cost but has to conform to headquarters' policies. Finally, inventories can be adjusted up to a certain point, in view of price increases as a result of devaluation and the current inflation. All these operations must be accomplished at a minimum risk and expected cost, without violating any of the Brazilian foreign-exchange controls.

4.2 Devaluation Outlook
Previous to the period in which this example is set, the economist of the Brazilian subsidiary studied the probable situation of the cruzeiro over the forthcoming 9 months. Four estimates were requested from him for each month: the probability of a devaluation, its most likely value, its highest possible value, and its lowest possible value. His conclusions can be summarized in a graph (Figure 4.1) and a table (Table 4.1). He comments on these data:

The next 5 months are dominated by the critically important coffee crop. The domination of this staple in the export picture of the country puts it in a position to create a balance of payment crisis all by itself. There is about a 50-50 probability that this crop will be bad, in which case a mild devaluation (13%) can be expected 3 months from now (see Figure 4.1). The chances of a devaluation next month are practically nil. Furthermore, after the critical third month, the probability of a devaluation levels off. From the sixth month on, another story starts. If the mild devaluation as a result of the coffee crop

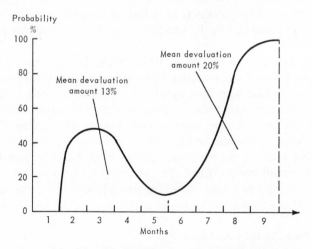

FIGURE 4.1   Monthly Devaluation Probabilities in Brazil

does not occur, an accumulation of balance of payment problems is expected in the ninth month. Government expenditures and the budgetary deficit fan the current inflation rate to unusual levels. With an inflation level of over 30%, a more serious devaluation (20%) can be forecast with virtual certainty about the end of the planning period.

Obviously, the further I look into the future, the less accurate my predictions are. This explains the increasing spread between the possible maximum and minimum amounts of the devaluation (see Table 4.1). I do not expect, of course, both devaluations to occur, but, as it is impossible to forecast at this time which one is actually going to happen, we should protect ourselves against both possibilities.

From the information of Table 4.1, a computer generator makes the computations and directly punches out the cards required for the quadratic programming code.[3]

Some permanent parameters are also required: namely, the correlations of probabilities and amounts of the devaluations over time. These correlations take into account the tendency of probabilities or amounts to move in unison. For instance, the economist's forecast of 13% as the most likely amount of the devaluation in the second month is wrong and should really be 16%. It is very likely that the third month's estimate should also be revised upward. If this new estimate was moving exactly in unison with the second month's estimate, a perfect positive correlation would exist (correlation factor equals one). This is exactly the assumption that was made: All devaluation amounts are perfectly positively correlated.

TABLE 4.1   Monthly Devaluation Probabilities and Possible Amounts

Month	Probability (%)	Most Likely Amount (%)	Maximum Amount (%)	Minimum Amount (%)
1	0	13	13	13
2	40	13	14	12
3	50	13	15	11
4	30	13	17	10
5	10	13	20	10
6	10	20	22	10
7	35	20	26	15
8	90	20	30	15
9	100	20	32	15

3. This generator is a subroutine of the full problem generator described in Chapter 7.

The correlation system of the probabilities was not assumed as automatic. The correlation factor of the devaluation probability of any month, with the one immediately following, was evaluated at 0.75. The impact of an error in probability estimates is even lower on the forecast of 2 months later (correlation factor equals 0.50) or the forecast of 3 months later (correlation factor equals 0.25). The effect on still later periods is negligible (correlation factor equals zero). In summary, an error in probability estimates has an impact on later periods' probabilities; this error levels off gradually and disappears after 4 months.

Clearly, these "permanent parameters" can be changed according to the management's judgment of the economic reality. More refined assumptions can be made and expressed mathematically,[4] but in the Ace International case the aim is to present only the basic model.

4.3 Framework of the Ace International Problem

The theoretical multitemporal model can be expressed as the problem of maximizing $Z = L$ (linear part) − quadratic part, subject to cost equations, profit equations, cash equations, exposure equations, and all other constraints.

In the linear part of the objective function appear the effective costs or returns of all the transactions. The quadratic part, measuring the risk, includes all the variances and covariances of the financing and hedging decisions. The cost equations compute the cost outlays resulting from all the transactions. The profit equations relate to profits realized by short-term financial transactions, such as treasury bills purchased with excess cash. The cash equations take care of the financial implications of all the transactions: cash requirements, cash inflows and outflows. The exposure equations deal with the impact of each transaction on the net exposure. For each month, there is one cost equation, one profit equation, one cash equation, and one exposure equation. "All other constraints" are the constraints imposed by company or government policy, and the specific constraints applicable to each transaction. Later sections will deal with these other constraints. We will focus now on the cost and profit, cash, and exposure equations.

4.3.1 *Cost and Profit Equations*

Although these equations are not indispensable for the model, they help in interpreting the results. All financing and hedging costs incurred

---

4. For example, if the probability of the 13% devaluation in months 1 to 5 increases, the probability of the second devaluation should decrease. A negative correlation system between the probability estimates of months 1 to 5 with the forecasts of months 6 to 9 could include these assumptions. See Section 6.1 for details.

are computed separately for each month. It is assumed that costs are accrued monthly. For example, a bank loan outstanding from months 1 to 3, inclusively, will create an interest expense in month 1, 2, and 3 separately, even when the total interest is due only at maturity.

There will be one cost equation for each month. In addition, the costs incurred "beyond the time horizon" are also calculated. These costs refer to interest expenses on other costs that will be due in periods later than the ninth month but which relate to decisions made within the time horizon. For instance, a 3 month bank loan initiated in month 9 will accrue interest expenses for 2 more months. These expenses, although incurred beyond the time horizon, are really decided within this time horizon and are therefore computed as part of the total costs. A last cost equation is simply the sum of all the monthly costs and the costs beyond the horizon.

The profit equations are, similarly, computations of profits accrued each month. In the Ace International case, the only sources of profits are treasury bond operations (see Section 4.10). Again each month's profits are computed separately, as well as a total profit figure for the entire time horizon.

4.3.2 Cash Equations

The cash equation has a set of variables and a constant term. The constant term represents what is defined as "basic cash requirements." These are funds whose need has been determined outside the model. The need for credit installments, for example, is determined by marketing considerations and is not a decision variable in the model. All other fund flows that are not considered as decision variables in the model are also basic cash requirements.

The treasurer prepares the basic cash requirements forecast for the 9 months in question. (See Table 4.2.) This is in fact a cash budget before interest expenses on new local loans, deposits for new forward exchange contracts or swap contracts, repatriation of profits, and excess inventory purchases.[5]

The total receipts are basically collections of accounts and notes receivable. Inventories are raw materials purchased during the month for the production process. They are calculated on the basis of economic order quantities, taking into account expected price increases (see Section 4.12). Manufacturing expenses are all the costs related to production. Operating expenses are administrative overhead, marketing, and distribution expenses. Taxes are due in three installments of increasing size during months 4 to 6. Two fixed assets purchases are

5. The exact meanings of these terms are to be found in Sections 3.5 to 3.12.

TABLE 4.2 Basic Cash Requirements of Ace International (in millions of cruzeiros at present exchange rate)

	Month 1	Month 2	Month 3	Month 4	Month 5	Month 6	Month 7	Month 8	Month 9
Total Receipts	(2,250)	(4,070)	(2,700)	(3,400)	(3,100)	(3,825)	(2,900)	(3,800)	(4,000)
Inventories	600	700	600	400	600	500	300	600	700
Manufacturing Expenses	1,500	1,600	1,800	1,850	1,900	1,950	2,000	2,000	2,100
Operating Expenses	1,600	1,300	1,400	1,400	1,600	1,600	1,800	1,900	2,000
Taxes				800	1,200	2,100			
Other Disbursements	1,200	1,300	4,200	150	1,300	1,300	1,250	1,300	1,200
Purchase of Fixed Assets				600				1,200	
Old Swap Repayments		1,500		1,800		1,600	1,600		1,400
Old Loan Repayments	1,000	2,000	3,000	1,000		500		500	
Interest Expenses on Outstanding Loans	200	185	70	40	30	25	20	20	20
Basic Cash Requirements	3,850	4,515	8,370	4,640	3,530	5,750	4,070	3,720	3,420

planned in months 4 and 8. The next three items correspond to fund flow commitments from earlier periods. Swap agreements concluded in previous months expire during the present planning period, creating mandatory cash outflows which have to be budgeted. Old debt repayment and interest costs on debt outstanding from months before our planning period create similar requirements.

All basic cash outflows minus total receipts will be considered the basic cash requirements. These basic cash requirements determine the constant term of each cash equation. The variables represent all the cash flows created by the decision variables of the model. For example, a bank loan will create a cash inflow in the month in which it is received, cash outflows for each interest payment, and a final outflow at maturity. Therefore, the general pattern of a cash equation is: Cash equals minus basic cash requirements plus variable inflows minus variable outflows. The model will not allow cash to become negative. In other words, all the cash requirements, basic or variables, have to be met. If the inflows exceed the total requirements, the net balance will be accumulated in cash.

4.3.3 Exposure Equations
The pattern of the exposure equations is similar to that of the cash equation. The constant term now represents the basic net exposure. It is part of the total exposure that is not a decision variable in the model.

The treasurer prepares a forecast of the basic exposure for the 9-month planning period (Table 4.3). This represents the exposed assets and exposed liabilities that escape his control at this time. The bulk of the exposed assets are the accounts receivable from installment sales. The exposed part of inventories is determined by a technique that will be described in Section 4.3.4. The largest items in exposed liabilities are accounts payable and old local debt outstanding.

The exposure equations will be of the type: Net exposure equals basic net exposure plus variable exposed assets minus variable exposed liabilities. If the model is prohibited from speculating on a currency devaluation, the net exposure cannot become negative.

4.3.4 Computation of Exposure of Inventories
One of the more difficult problems in accounting for devaluation is inventory reporting: Are inventories of raw materials, work in process, and finished goods exposed assets? As mentioned earlier, the major accounting authorities have differing opinions. The Accounting Research Bulletin decides that inventories are 100% exposed assets.

TABLE 4.3 Basic Net Exposure of Ace International (in millions of cruzeiros at present exchange rate)

	Month 1	Month 2	Month 3	Month 4	Month 5	Month 6	Month 7	Month 8	Month 9
Accounts and Notes Receivable	12,500	13,000	14,000	15,000	15,500	15,000	16,000	14,000	18,000
Exposed Part of Inventories	2,600	2,800	3,000	3,000	3,500	3,000	4,000	4,000	4,500
All Other Basic Exposed Assets	6,000	6,500	6,000	6,500	6,500	6,000	6,500	7,000	7,000
Accounts and Notes Payable	(6,000)	(7,000)	(7,000)	(6,000)	(7,000)	(7,500)	(7,000)	(6,000)	(7,000)
Old Debt Outstanding	(10,000)	(9,000)	(8,000)	(4,000)	(3,000)	(3,000)	(2,500)	(2,000)	(2,000)
Taxes Payable	(2,000)	(2,000)	(3,000)	(4,100)	(3,300)	(2,100)			
Basic Net Exposure	3,100	4,300	5,000	10,400	12,200	11,400	17,000	17,000	20,500

The National Accounting Association claims that inventories are completely unexposed. The position of this paper is that inventories can be all the way from 100% exposed to 100% negatively exposed or any value in between including 0% exposed. Here, inventories of a product are exposed when the dollar market value decreases more than the dollar replacement costs after a devaluation. In other words, the "dollar profit margin" on inventories as defined by the difference between market value and replacement value is the key variable to define the degree of exposure.

The percentage of exposure of inventories of a specific product is determined by the formula:

$$e = \frac{Y - X}{IW}$$

where

e = percentage of exposure of inventory;
X = dollar replacement value decrease after a devaluation;
Y = dollar market value decrease after a devaluation;
I = book value of inventories; and
W = expected devaluation amount.

The use of this formula compares well with the intuitive concept of exposure. This is best understood by taking some extreme examples.

Let us assume a given product with a book value of $100 and a 20% expected devaluation amount ($I = \$100$ and $W = 0.20$; therefore the denominator of the formula is always $20). Inventories of the product are 100% exposed when all inputs are imported, and the output is destined to the local market where price freezing is effective.

In this case, the dollar replacement value is not changed by a devaluation ($X = 0$) and the proceeds from sales in the local market will be reduced by $20 ($Y = \$20$). The exposure formula yields 20/20 = 100%. In contrast, no exposure will prevail if all inputs and outputs are imports and exports, respectively. Again, the dollar replacement value is unaffected ($X = 0$), but this time the dollar market will not change either ($Y = 0$).

A similar case develops if all inputs and outputs are local, and the government price freezing is equally effective (or ineffective) in controlling both. In this case $X = Y$, and again the formula would show an exposure of 0%.

It is possible to imagine cases in which inventories are negatively exposed (that is, reduce the net exposure of the affiliate). For instance, if all inputs are local products and the government price freezing is effective ($X = \$20$) and the output is sold abroad or in a local market without price controls ($Y = 0$), the inventories are 100% negatively exposed. In other words, abnormally high dollar profit margins are possible, and the sale of the inventories after the devaluation would yield a much higher dollar profit than before the devaluation. Obviously, only rarely will companies have inventories in any one of these extreme cases.

An example classifies how it is possible to handle less extreme and more complex problems: A given product is produced simultaneously for the local and export markets. It has a content of imported raw materials, local raw materials, and local labor.

The following assumptions are made:

The expected devaluation of the cruzeiro is 20%.

The dollar prices and amounts in the export market do not change after the devaluation.

The government will be successful at freezing the price level of the product at 100 cruzeiros after the devaluation.

After the devaluation, some of the imported raw materials will be replaced by the cheaper local raw materials.

The cruzeiro price of the local raw materials will increase by 5% after the devaluation.

The average labor costs in cruzeiros will inflate by 10% after the devaluation.

The book value of the inventories is the replacement value before the devaluation.

The analysis of the dollar market value and the dollar replacement value determines an exposure of 27.11% on the inventories of this product, as computed in Table 4.4. It is by an analysis of this type, by product or by product group, that the "exposed part of inventories" was computed in Table 4.3.

4.4 Notation

In the Ace International problem, all variables are identified by a set of letters followed by a month number:

CSH 1 represents the net cash in the first month.

EXP 4 represents the net exposure in the fourth month.[6]

BLA 8 represents a bank loan, type A, available in the eighth month. (Detailed definition of the different types of loans is given in Section 4.5.1.)

6. The variables EXP k are identical to the values X_{N+k} used in the theoretical formulation in the previous chapters. From now on, only EXP k will be used.

TABLE 4.4 Market and Replacement Value Analysis

	Before Devaluation (100 Cruzeiros = $)				After Devaluation (125 Cruzeiros = $1)			
	Units (Mil.)	Price Per Unit (cruzeiros)	Price Per Unit ($)	Total $ Value (Mil.)	Units (Mil.)	Price Per Unit (cruzeiros)	Price Per Unit ($)	Total $ Value (Mil.)
Market Value								
Export Sales	2.0	100	$1.0	$2.0	2.0	125	$1.0	$2.0
Local Sales	3.0	100	1.0	3.0	3.0	100	0.8	2.4
Total				$5.0				$4.4
				$Y = \$600,000$				
Replacement Value								
Imported Raw Materials	1.0	200	$2.0	$2.0	0.95	250	$2.0	$1.9
Local Raw Materials	0.5	200	$2.0	$1.0	0.55	210	$1.68	$0.924
Local Labor Input (man-hours)	0.5	300	$3.0	$1.5	0.50	330	$2.64	$1.32
Total				$4.5				$4.144
				$X = \$356,000$				

$$e = \frac{Y - X}{ID} = \frac{\$600,000 - \$356,000}{\$4,500,000 \times 20\%} = 27.11\%$$

CST k represents the financing and hedging costs incurred in period k.

CST* represents the financing and hedging costs beyond the time horizon.

COST represents the total financing and hedging costs over the nine months.

PRT k represents the profit realized on bond transactions in period k.

PROF represents the total profit over the 9 months.

As examples, some cost, profit, cash, and exposure equations are schematically presented:

$$\text{CST } k = \text{sum of other terms} \cdots.$$

$$\text{COST} = \sum_{k=1}^{9} \text{CST } k + \text{CST*}.$$

$$\text{PRT } k = \cdots \text{sum of other terms} \cdots.$$

$$\text{PROF} = \sum_{k=1}^{9} \text{PRT } k.$$

$$\text{CSH } 1 = -3,850 \text{ Million} \cdots + (\text{other terms}) \cdots;$$
$$\text{CSH } 2 = -4,515 \text{ Million} \cdots + (\text{other terms}) \cdots;$$
$$\text{CSH } 3 = -5,370 \text{ Million} \cdots + (\text{other terms}) \cdots;$$
$$\text{EXP } 1 = 3,100 \text{ Million} \cdots + (\text{other terms}) \cdots;$$
$$\text{EXP } 2 = 4,300 \text{ Million} \cdots + (\text{other terms}) \cdots;$$
$$\text{EXP } 3 = 5,000 \text{ Million} \cdots + (\text{other terms}) \cdots;$$

and so forth. The "other terms" are made up of variables of the model.

The framework of the Ace International case, as presented in Section 4.3, can now be expressed with more precision:

Objective function[7]

$$\text{maximize } Z = L(\text{PROF} - \text{COST} - \sum_{k=1}^{9} A_{N+k} \text{EXP } k)$$

$$- \sum_{k-1}^{9} V_{N+k}(\text{EXP } k)^2 + (\text{other quadratic terms})$$

subject to:

Cost equation

$$\text{COST} = \sum_{k=1}^{9} \text{CST } k + \text{CST*};$$

where $\text{CST } k = \cdots (\text{other terms}) \cdots, \quad k = 1, \ldots, 9,$

7. A_{N+k} = Devaluation coefficient of period k (see Chapter 3); it represents the product of the devaluation probability and the expected devaluation amount. V_{N+k} = variance of devaluation coefficient of period k.

Profit equation

$$PROF = \sum_{k=1}^{9} PRT\ k;$$

where   PRT $k = \cdots$ (other terms) $\cdots$, $k = 1, \ldots 9$,

Cash equation

CSH $k =$ (basic cash requirement) $+ \cdots$ (other terms), $k = 1, \ldots, 9$;

Exposure equation

EXP $k =$ (basic net exposure) $+ \cdots$ (other terms), $k = 1, \ldots, 9$;

all other constraints.

In the balance of this chapter, all the "other terms" and "other constraints" will be analyzed.

4.5   Available Local Loans

Two different types of loans are considered: bank loans in general and private loans. Bank loans can always be obtained. The amounts available to Ace International at each price fluctuate, but it is always possible to raise funds, at a high cost. Private loans are more volatile in their availability. Another large Brazilian company has a temporary excess cash position and decides to make this cash available as a private loan to Ace International. The terms of these offers are rather unpredictable and are available only for a few weeks on a take-or-leave basis. All these loans have in common their complete vulnerability to a devaluation. (Pegging a loan to a price index is illegal in Brazil.) They will all behave like an exposed liability (see Figure 4.2)

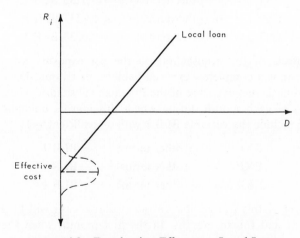

FIGURE 4.2   Devaluation Effect on a Local Loan

4.5.1 *Bank Loans*

The nominal interest rate of all the bank loans in Brazil is identical: the legal maximum of 12%. However, this interest rate is completely irrelevant. The Brazilian banks invariably require compensating balances, payment of interest at the initiation of the loan, special charges, and so forth; these requirements bring the effective interest rate much higher.

How is a local loan included in the model? For example, a loan is available in the first month, with a probable effective cost of 28% per annum. The exact terms of this loan are not completely known yet, but the effective cost is between 32% and 24%. This allows the calculation of the variance ($V = 0.000178$). Interest and principal are payable after 3 months. Here, this bank loan is called Type *B*, with notation BLB 1. This variable BLB 1 will appear in the model in the objective function and in a number of constraints as described later.

In the objective function, the contribution of the variance of this transaction to the strategy risk is handled by including the square of BLB 1 multiplied by its variance.

The objective function is

$$\text{maximize } Z = \cdots \text{(other terms)} \cdots - 0.000178 \text{ (BLB 1)}^2$$

The cost of this loan is incorporated in the cost equations of each month during which the loan is outstanding. The coefficient of the variable is the expected monthly interest expense ($0.28/12 = 0.0233$).

As the loan is outstanding during the three first months, the variable appears in the three corresponding cost equations:

$$\text{CST } 1 = \cdots \text{(other terms)} \cdots + 0.0233 \text{ BLB 1}$$
$$\text{CST } 2 = \cdots \text{(other terms)} \cdots + 0.0233 \text{ BLB 1}$$
$$\text{CST } 3 = \cdots \text{(other terms)} \cdots + 0.0233 \text{ BLB 1}$$

The effects of this transaction on the net exposure are obvious. As this loan is a completely exposed liability, its amount has to be deducted from the net exposure of the Brazilian subsidiary. The exposure equations of each month during which this loan is outstanding will therefore include the variable BLB 1 with a coefficient -1;

$$\text{EXP } 1 = \cdots \text{(other terms)} \cdots - \text{BLB 1}$$
$$\text{EXP } 2 = \cdots \text{(other terms)} \cdots - \text{BLB 1}$$
$$\text{EXP } 3 = \cdots \text{(other terms)} \cdots - \text{BLB 1}$$

The impact of this transaction on the available cash will be apparent in the first and fourth months. In the first month, when the loan is initiated, the amount of the loan will cause an inflow of cash. In the corresponding cash equation the variable will appear with a coefficient $+1$. On the other hand, at the termination of the loan, the repayment of the principal and interest causes a cash outflow. The variable BLB 1 appears in the cash equation of the fourth month (the repayment is due on the first day of the fourth month), with a coefficient -1.07, because a cumulated 7% of interest expenses is due at that time. The cash equations that involve BLB 1 are therefore:

$$\text{CSH } 1 = \cdots \text{(other terms)} \cdots + \text{BLB } 1$$
$$\text{CSH } 4 = \cdots \text{(other terms)} \cdots - 1.07 \text{ BLB } 1$$

If the interest was payable monthly, the cash constraints would be:

$$\text{CSH } 1 = \cdots \text{(other terms)} \cdots + \text{BLB } 1$$
$$\text{CSH } 2 = \cdots \text{(other terms)} \cdots - 0.0233 \text{ BLB } 1$$
$$\text{CSH } 3 = \cdots \text{(other terms)} \cdots - 0.0233 \text{ BLB } 1$$
$$\text{CSH } 4 = \cdots \text{(other terms)} \cdots - 1.0233 \text{ BLB } 1$$

and no changes in the other equations. In this fashion, all types of repayment schedules and interest rates can be introduced in the model.

In a real-life problem solved by the model, the number of loan variables was 109, which would unduly complicate the exposition at this point. The problem is simplified by assuming that all bank loans have a similar repayment schedule: principal and interest are payable after 3 months.

One should bear in mind that each of those loans is not necessarily drawn from a single bank. A loan from bank X with a compensating balance and another one available at bank Y, with special charges, can have the same effective interest rate. In this model, they are put together. We will distinguish between bank loans Types A, B, C, and D.

BANK LOAN TYPE A (BLA k)   These are the cheapest bank loans available during period k. The mean effective interest cost is 22%, with the extreme points of the distribution at 20% and 24% variance = 0.0000435). Only a very limited amount of those loans are available.

BANK LOAN TYPE B (BLB k)   The average effective interest rate is 28% with fluctuation between 24% and 32% (variance = 0.000178). The amount available at these rates is fluctuating between 1.4 billion and 1.9 billion cruzeiros during the next 9 months.

BANK LOAN TYPE C (BLC k)   Effective interest rate is 36% with a spread between 32% and 41% (variance = 0.000225). Roughly 5,200 million cruzeiros are available at all times at this cost.

BANK LOAN TYPE D (BLD k)   Effective interest rate is 45.5% with a spread between 41% and 50% (variance = 0.000625). At all times, a virtually unlimited supply is available at this price.

Each one of these loans will be incorporated in the model in a fashion similar to the example of BLB 1. In addition to the equations already explained, these variables will appear in the model in a number of other constraints. A first group of such constraints corresponds to the ceilings on the available amounts on each transaction, as shown in Table 4.5. Each variable will therefore appear in the maximum constraint, of which some examples are

$$\text{BLA } 1 \le 870 \text{ million cruzeiros}$$
$$\text{BLB } 1 \le 1{,}700 \text{ million cruzeiros}$$
$$\text{BLB } 2 \le 1{,}900 \text{ million cruzeiros}$$
$$\text{BLC } 6 \le 5{,}200 \text{ million cruzeiros}$$

TABLE 4.5   Maximum Amounts on Bank Loans (In Millions of Constant Cruzeiros)

Month k	BLA	BLB	BLC	BLD
1	870	1,700	5,200	∞
2	1,000	1,900	5,200	∞
3	600	1,700	5,200	∞
4	900	1,700	5,200	∞
5	700	1,700	5,200	∞
6	700	1,500	5,200	∞
7	600	1,400	5,200	∞
8	500	1,400	5,200	∞
9	500	1,400	5,200	∞

A second group of constraints relates to a policy decision. For instance, suppose that Ace International has the policy of keeping a minimum of 4 billion cruzeiros in outstanding bank loans in Brazil. The purpose of this policy is to keep the lines of credit open for emergencies. This decision is translated into mathematical form as a minimum constraint on total bank loans outstanding:

Constraint for month 1:

BLA 1 + BLB 1 + BLC 1 + BLD 1
    + (old debt outstanding in month 1) ≥ 4,000 million cruzeiros.

Constraint for month 2:

BLA 1 + BLB 1 + BLC 1 + BLD 1 + BLA 2 + BLB 2 + BLC 2
+ BLD 2 (old debt outstanding in month 2) ≥ 4,000 million cruzeiros.

Constraint for month k:

$$\sum_{i=k-3}^{k} (\text{BLA } k + \text{BLB } k + \text{BLC } k + \text{BLD } k)$$
    + (old debt outstanding in month k) ≥ 4,000 million cruzeiros.

4.5.2 Private Loans
Only three private loans during the 9 month period are considered:

PRIVATE LOAN A (PLA 1).   This loan is available in the first month, at an effective interest of 2% per month, interest payable each month. Maturity is at 6 months. Total amount available: 1,260 million cruzeiros. The variance of the interest cost is relatively high because of the unpredictable nature of the final agreement (variance 0.0016).

PRIVATE LOAN B (PLB 4).   This loan is payable, interest and principal, after 4 months, and has an effective cost of 29% with a variance of 0.0014. Total amount is 600 million cruzeiros.

PRIVATE LOAN C (PLC 7).   This is a short-term loan of only 1 month but at a very interesting annualized effective interest cost of 16% (variance 0.002). Total amount available, 1,400 million cruzeiros.

Only the incorporation of PLA 1 into the model will be shown. The others can be introduced by analogy. The objective function is

maximize $Z = \cdots$ (other terms) $\cdots - 0.0016 \,(\text{PLA } 1)^2$

Subject to:

CST 1 = $\cdots$ (other terms) $\cdots + 0.02$ (PLA 1)
CST 2 = $\cdots$ (other terms) $\cdots + 0.02$ (PLA 1)
CST 3 = $\cdots$ (other terms) $\cdots + 0.02$ (PLA 1)
CST 4 = $\cdots$ (other terms) $\cdots + 0.02$ (PLA 1)
CST 5 = $\cdots$ (other terms) $\cdots + 0.02$ (PLA 1)
CSH 1 = $\cdots$ (other terms) $\cdots +$ PLA 1

$$\text{CSH } 2 = \cdots \text{(other terms)} \cdots - 0.02 \text{ (PLA 1)}$$
$$\text{CSH } 3 = \cdots \text{(other terms)} \cdots - 0.02 \text{ (PLA 1)}$$
$$\text{CSH } 4 = \cdots \text{(other terms)} \cdots - 0.02 \text{ (PLA 1)}$$
$$\text{CSH } 5 = \cdots \text{(other terms)} \cdots - 0.02 \text{ (PLA 1)}$$
$$\text{CSH } 6 = \cdots \text{(other terms)} \cdots - 1.02 \text{ (PLA 1)}$$
$$\text{EXP } 1 = \cdots \text{(other terms)} \cdots - \text{PLA 1}$$
$$\text{EXP } 2 = \cdots \text{(other terms)} \cdots - \text{PLA 1}$$
$$\text{EXP } 3 = \cdots \text{(other terms)} \cdots - \text{PLA 1}$$
$$\text{EXP } 4 = \cdots \text{(other terms)} \cdots - \text{PLA 1}$$
$$\text{EXP } 5 = \cdots \text{(other terms)} \cdots - \text{PLA 1}$$

PLA $1 \le 1{,}260$ million cruzeiros.

4.6 Straight Dollar Loans From New York Headquarters

Whenever local financing is not available or too expensive, the Brazilian subsidiary can import dollars from New York. The cost of these loans is fairly stable, but they do not change the exposure of the Brazilian subsidiary.

The effective cost of a dollar loan is the effective cost of the loan in the United States, plus the spread between buy and sell prices of the cruzeiro, plus the transactions cost. This total is 11.1 %. None of those costs is expected to vary seriously in the 9-month period (variance = 0). The repayment is scheduled beyond the time horizon of 9 months. For the magnitudes considered here, an unlimited amount of dollars can be supplied from New York. The symbol for straight dollar loans will be S\$L k. It is assumed again that all maturities are identical: for instance, 10 months.

The introduction of these variables in the model is very simple. They will appear in the cost equations with a coefficient representing the monthly interest expense. There is no variance, no exposure effect, no maximum constraints, or any other constraints.

The cash effect is simply the inflow during the month in which the dollar loan is initiated. As the repayment is due beyond the time horizon, no outflows have to be budgeted in the model. For variable S\$L 1, for example, the only constraints are:

$$\text{CST } k = \cdots \text{(other terms)} \cdots + 0.00917 \text{ S\$L 1} \qquad k = 1, \ldots, 9,$$
$$\text{CSH } 1 = \cdots \text{(other terms)} \cdots + \text{S\$L 1}$$

4.7 Forward-Exchange Contracts

A forward-exchange contract can be defined as "an operation in exchange whereby a rate is fixed at once for a purchase or sale of one currency for another which is to be completed at some future date."[9] Forward markets have been developing vigorously since World War II. In prewar days, a 6-month futures contract was difficult to obtain and one for more than 12 months almost impossible. Today, yearly contracts are routine in the major world currencies and arrangements are made for up to 7 years.

Covering the exchange risk of an export or import transaction is complicated if the exact date of the final transaction is not known. Shipping or manufacturing delays modify the date of payment. For this reason, optional forward exchange contracts are available. "They usually assume the form of contracts with the maximum and minimum time limits between which the currency sold is to be delivered or between which the delivery of the currency bought is to be taken."[10] Another system, practiced only in the United States, is a contract specifying a set of alternative dates at which the option can be exercised, with different exchange rates fixed for each date.

To demonstrate the versatility of the model, the forward-exchange conditions existing in Brazil during 1966 are chosen. Government control is making the forward cruzeiro contract a fairly complex operation. The right to buy futures is subject to very specific conditions, defined under the Brazilian "SUMOC 289" loan regulation.[11] The full operation includes:

1. Import from abroad of a hard-currency loan (dollars can be assumed). This loan had to "qualify," that is, be recognized as contributing to the industrial development of Brazil.
2. These incoming dollars can be remitted — at the normal remittance cost — within 30 days after the import date.
3. The government guarantees the right to buy forward-exchange contracts after these 30 days and before 90 days, at the free market rate.
4. A deposit of 20% of the total contract is required in dollars, at the date of the exercise of the option. This deposit is not interest

9. Herbert Edwin Evitt and W. W. Syrett, *A Manual of Foreign Exchange*, 6th ed. by W. W. Syrett (London; Pitman Publishing Corp., 1966). p. 144.

10. Paul A. Einzig, *A Textbook on Foreign Exchange* (New York: St. Martin's Press, 1966), Chapter 4.

11. We changed some conditions of the "SUMOC 289" loans for this presentation, especially the time periods involved.

bearing and is not covered by the future contract. The contract covers 3 months calculated from the day of the deposit.

5. At the time of the remittance of the funds, the 80% balance is payable in cruzeiros, with a 1.5% monthly interest cost on this balance.

An example will clarify the transactions. Ace International succeeded in qualifying a straight dollar loan from the headquarters for its manufacturing subsidiary as a "SUMOC 289" loan. The date this loan cleared in Brazil is January 1. For 1 month, these funds will remain unprotected against a cruzeiro depreciation. From February 1 to April 1, Ace International has the option to buy a future contract. If the treasurer decides to exercise the option as soon as possible, the transaction will be as in Figure 4.3.

On February 1, a 20% deposit in dollars is made at the Banco do Brasil. Three months later, on May 1, a payment of 80% of the contract and an interest cost of 3.6% (that is, $3 \times 1.5 \times 0.8$) is added. The dollars, at the forward contract price, are made available at the headquarters in the United States. If the option were exercised at the latest possible date, April 1, the deposit would be made on that date. The final remittance would then occur on July 1.

The foregoing presentation does not discuss the element listed earlier in this section as Number 2 in the initial breakdown of the operation: the possibility of remitting the loan at the normal remittance cost, within 30 days after the import date. This clause allows a complete turnabout of the funds. One can raise funds at the same time in Brazil and New York, get a qualification, swap the loans, and obtain the right to buy futures (Figure 4.4). The advantage of this technique is that the dollars are not exposed between the reception of the dollar loan and the exercise of the option. The forward-exchange contract can then be used to cover exposed assets. The disadvantage is the cash drain it represents. The net cash flow of the "reception of the loan" is

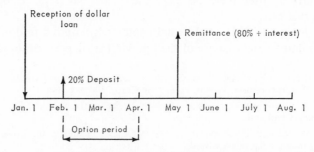

FIGURE 4.3   Cash Flow for Forward Exchange Contract without Turnabout

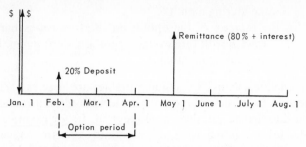

FIGURE 4.4 Cash Flow for Forward Exchange Contract with Turnabout

nil (funds coming in equal outgoing dollars). The 20% dollar deposit is still required, as is the 80% remittance with the interest expenses. If the Brazilian subsidiary has an excess cash position, this scheme is easy to implement. If not, it will be forced to raise money in the local (and expensive) capital market.

The treasurer has, therefore, to take into account the dates on which a qualified loan is received, and the cash position and capital market condition on those dates, to decide between a turnaround operation or a straight dollar loan. Exposure and the probability of a cruzeiro depreciation are other factors in influencing the decision. Finally, he has to budget the 20% deposit and the final remittances. The whole operation is to be timed to guarantee coverage at the critical devaluation moment.

The treasurer knows that the production department intends to increase the capacity of the manufacturing facility. Qualification of a 700 million cruzeiro loan (*A*) in the second month, and another one of 1,600 million cruzeiros during the fourth month (*B*) is, therefore, practically certain.

How will all these operations be included in the model? Assume again that all transactions occur on the first day of the month in which they occur. The following definitions are needed:

FFA 3 = the exercise of the option on the forward exchange contract *A* (corresponding to the qualified loan *A* of month 2) without turnaround operation, during month 3.

FFA 4 = the exercise of the option on the forward-exchange contract *A*, without turnaround operation, during month 4.

FTA 3 = the exercise of the option on the forward-exchange con-contract *A*, with a turnaround operation, during month 3.

FTA 4 = same, during month 4.

FFB 5 = the exercise of the option on the forward-exchange contract *B* (corresponding to the qualified loan *B* of month 4) without turnaround operation, during month 5.

FFB 6 = same, during month 6.

FTB 5 = the exercise of the option on the forward-exchange contract B with turnaround operation, during month 5.

FTB 6 = same, during month 6.

For 2 qualified loans, 8 decision variables are necessary. This is a simplification from the reality: In a problem based on a real situation, 64 forward-exchange variables were required. If, for example, FFA 4 is included in the solution, what cash flows and exposure changes occur?

1. A net cash inflow of the qualified loan in month 2:

$$\text{CSH } 2 = \cdots \text{(other terms)} \cdots + \text{FFA } 4.$$

2. A 20% cash outflow for the deposit in month 4:

$$\text{CSH } 2 = \cdots \text{(other terms)} \cdots - 0.2 \text{ FFA } 4.$$

3. An outflow of 83.6% in month 7 (80% remittance + 3.6% interest):

$$\text{CSH } 7 = \cdots \text{(other terms)} \cdots - 0.836 \text{ FFA } 4.$$

4. The exposure of months 2 and 3 increases by the full amount:

$$\text{EXP } 2 = \cdots \text{(other terms)} \cdots + \text{FFA } 4;$$
$$\text{EXP } 3 = \cdots \text{(other terms)} \cdots + \text{FFA } 4.$$

5. The net exposure of month 4 to 7 is increased by 20% (the deposit is never protected):

$$\text{EXP } 4 = \cdots \text{(other terms)} \cdots + 0.2 \text{ FFA } 4;$$
$$\text{EXP } 5 = \cdots \text{(other terms)} \cdots + 0.2 \text{ FFA } 4;$$
$$\text{EXP } 6 = \cdots \text{(other terms)} \cdots + 0.2 \text{ FFA } 4.$$

If FTA 4 is considered in the solution, what will change in this five-step analysis?

1. No net cash inflow in month 2.
2. No change from FFA 4 example.
3. No change from FFA 4 example.
4. No exposure increase.
5. The net exposure of months 4 to 7 decreases by 80% of FTA 4:

$$\text{EXP } k = \cdots \text{(other terms)} \cdots - 0.8 \text{ FTA } 4, \qquad k = 4,5,6,7$$

An additional type of constraint is required by the forward-exchange operations. The option can only be exercised once, that is, if FFA 3 is chosen, the option cannot be taken a second time in the fourth month by including FFA 4 in the solution. In other words, FFA 3 and FFA 4 are mutually exclusive variables. This constraint is introduced through the "big M" artifice. In the objective function, the term $-M$(FFA 3)(FFA 4) is included, where M is a very large number. As the aim is to maximize the objective function, the introduction of both variables in the solution would be heavily penalized, and virtually impossible.

The variables FTA 3 and FTA 4 are also mutually exclusive; so are FTA 3 and FFA4, FFA3 and FTA 4. Note that it is possible, however, to have at the same time FFA 4 and FTA 4, or FFA 5 and FTA 5. This corresponds to a situation in which the straight dollar loan has only partially been turned around. The total option can still be exercised. Similar constraints are introduced, *mutatis mutandis*, for the variables corresponding to the qualified loan *B*.

A final constraint is that futures can only be bought on qualified loans:

FFA 3 + FFA 4 + FTA 3 + FTA 4 ≤ 700 million cruzeiros.

FFB 5 + FFB 6 + FTB 5 + FTB 6 ≤ 1,600 million cruzeiros.

For the cost equations, the annual interest rate of the future-exchange contract is needed. This cost is the sum of the effective cost of the dollar loan in the United States, the transactions cost, and the interest expense of the forward contract. The first 2 cost items are the same as in a straight dollar loan (total = 11.1%). The annualized interest cost of the contract is 14.4% ($12 \times 1.5 \times 0.8$). The total futures cost is, then, 25.5%. The characteristics of a forward-exchange decision variable can be presented graphically (Figures 4.5 and 4.6).

In summary, the forward exchange variable FFA 4, for instance, will appear in the following way:

1. The objective function is

   maximize $Z = \cdots$ (other terms) $\cdots$

   $$-M\text{(FFA 3)(FFA 4)} - M\text{(FTA 3)(FFA 4)}$$

2. Cost equation:

   CST $k = \cdots$ (other terms) $\cdots + 0.0212$ (FFA 4) $k = 4,5,6$

3. Cash constraint:

   CSH 2, CSH 4, CSH 7 as explained earlier.

4. Exposure constraint:

   EXP 2, EXP 4 to EXP 7 as explained previously

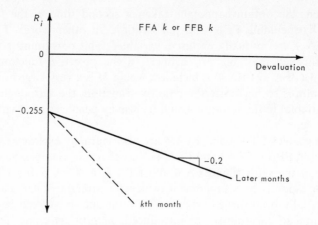

FIGURE 4.5   Devaluation Effect on Forward Exchange Contract
(FFA k or FFB k)

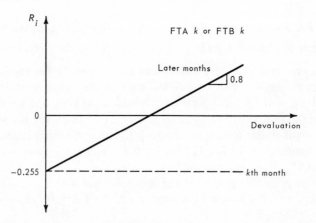

FIGURE 4.6   Devaluation Effect on Forward Exchange Contract
(FTA k or FTB k)

5. Maximum constraint:

FFA 3 + FFA 4 + FTA 3 + FTA $4 \leq 700$ million cruzeiros.

4.8 Swap Transactions

In international finance, the term "foreign-exchange swap" refers to a transaction in which equivalent amounts of 2 different currencies are swapped for a certain period. At the end of the swap period, both parties return the original amounts in each currency. Such transactions usually occur between a hard and a soft currency. The advantage for the swap taker, usually a bank in the soft currency country, is the cheap use of hard currency during the swap period. The swap creditor, who initiated the transaction, has the advantage of not being exposed to a soft currency depreciation during the swap period. In general, the hard currency deposit is not interest-bearing, while the soft currency loan is paying an interest charge.

Thus, the cost of a swap transaction is made up of 3 parts: (1) the interest opportunity cost of the hard currency deposit; (2) the interest charge on the soft currency loan; and (3) the conversion rate at which the soft currency funds are made available.

In the case of Brazil, swaps have been illegal since the 1965 devaluation. But simply to demonstrate how swaps can be included in the model, it is assumed that some swaps are still available.

There are different kinds of swap agreements.[12] A private swap is arranged with a private bank or institution in Brazil. These swaps tend to be more expensive and sometimes do not have a fixed rate of exchange. The borrower in this case has to arrange simultaneously a forward-exchange contract expiring the same day as the swap does. The more general case, an official swap, is a contract with the Banco do Brasil, and exchange rates are fixed. No future contract is necessary in this case.

Export swaps are specialized swaps to finance exports of goods. The exporter borrows, for example, $100,000 in hard currency abroad and deposits this currency in the Banco do Brasil for a loan in cruzeiros at a rate of 1,000 cr./$. He purchases his goods in Brazil with these cruzeiros. After the export of the goods, the exporter receives from his customers about $100,000, which is used to repay the original hard currency loan. By this time, the cruzeiro is at 1,200 cr./$, for instance. To settle the swap, the Banco do Brasil will pay the exporter an additional 20 million cruzeiros, reflecting the depreciation of the cruzeiros during the swap.

Ace International exports some parts made in Brazil to European subsidiaries. This entitles Ace International to export swaps with the Banco do Brasil. In addition, an official swap is available for a 6-month period.[13]

The financial swap is available during the second month. The

12. Guenter Reimann and Edwin F Wigglesworth, *The Challenge of International Finance* (New York: McGraw-Hill Book Co., Inc., 1966), p. 556.

13. This is an abnormally short financial swap. Normally, a swap contract covers a period of 360 days. Two-year contracts are also routine. Exceptionally, agreements over 5 years have been made.

maximum amount the Banco do Brasil is ready to swap with Ace International is 1000 million cruzeiros, at the official exchange rate of 2,200 cr./$. The free market rate at the same time is 2,640 cr./$, or 20% higher. The dollar deposit is non-interest-bearing, while the cruzeiros are made available at 10% per annum. Ace International borrows the dollars in the United States at 6.8%. An additional 2.5% is charged for general stamp taxes, brokerage fees, special contract stamps, and stock exchange commissions.

What is the total cost of this financial swap? The interest cost on the dollar loan in the United States applies to 120% of the swap transaction (because the company has to make available 20% more dollars than the cruzeiro equivalent received by the Brazilian subsidiary). The interest cost in the United States thus represents 8.16% (6.8% × 1.20). The total costs are:

Interest cost in United States	8.16%
Interest cost in Brazil	10.0%
Transaction cost	2.5%
	20.66%

The major variance in those costs is the result of the uncertainty of the free market rate. The treasurer feels that this rate could be as low as parity with the official rate, or as high as 40% over the official rate. We compute the variance of the swap cost on this basis (variance = 0.00001). An official swap, with fixed exchange rates, reduces the net exposure. These assumptions can be presented graphically in Figure 4.7.

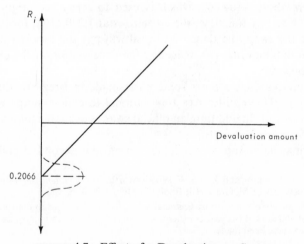

FIGURE 4.7   Effect of a Devaluation on Swaps

The cash effect is an inflow of cash in the month in which the swap agreement is made (month 2), and an outflow of the same amount and interest cost at the end of the contract. A clause in the contract provides that Ace International has the option to settle up to 50% of the swap contract after 3 months. Define:

FSW 2 = amount of the total swap agreement accepted during the second month.

SSW 5 = amount of optional settlement three months after the initiation of the swap.

SSW 8 = balance of swap settlement.

The constraints on these variables are

maximum amount of swap contract = FSW $2 \leq 1,000$ million cruzeiros.

settlements equal total swap contract: SSW 5 + SSW 8 = FSW 2.

maximum amount of optional settlement = SSW $5 \leq 0.5$ FSW 2.

These variables will also appear in the cost, exposure, and cash constraints and the objective function: The objective function is

$$\text{maximize } Z = \cdots \text{(other terms)} \cdots - 0.00001 \text{ (FSW 2)}^2$$

Cost equations:

$$\text{CST 2} = \cdots \text{(other terms)} \cdots + 0.0172 \text{ FSW 2}$$
$$\text{CST 3} = \cdots \text{(other terms)} \cdots + 0.0172 \text{ FSW 2}$$
$$\text{CST 4} = \cdots \text{(other terms)} \cdots + 0.0172 \text{ FSW 2}$$
$$\text{CST 5} = \cdots \text{(other terms)} \cdots + 0.0172 \text{ FSW 2} - 0.0172 \text{ SSW 5}$$
$$\text{CST 6} = \cdots \text{(other terms)} \cdots + 0.0172 \text{ FSW 2} - 0.0172 \text{ SSW 5}$$
$$\text{CST 7} = \cdots \text{(other terms)} \cdots + 0.0172 \text{ FSW 2} - 0.0172 \text{ SSW 5}$$

Cash equations:

$$\text{CSH 2} = \cdots \text{(other terms)} \cdots + \text{FSW 2}$$
$$\text{CSH 5} = \cdots \text{(other terms)} \cdots - 1.0425 \text{ SSW 5}$$
$$\text{CSH 8} = \cdots \text{(other terms)} \cdots - 1.085 \text{ SSW 8}$$

Exposure equations:

$$\text{EXP 2} = \cdots \text{(other terms)} \cdots - \text{FSW 2}$$
$$\text{EXP 3} = \cdots \text{(other terms)} \cdots - \text{FSW 2}$$
$$\text{EXP 4} = \cdots \text{(other terms)} \cdots - \text{FSW 2}$$
$$\text{EXP 5} = \cdots \text{(other terms)} \cdots - \text{FSW 2} + \text{SSW 5}$$
$$\text{EXP 6} = \cdots \text{(other terms)} \cdots - \text{FSW 2} + \text{SSW 5}$$
$$\text{EXP 7} = \cdots \text{(other terms)} \cdots - \text{FSW 2} + \text{SSW 5}$$

In the cost equations, when the financial swap is accepted, a monthly interest expense of 1.72% is incurred. These costs would be reduced from the fifth month on by the amount of the optional settlement.

We will now analyze the export swap Ace International can obtain in connection with the export of parts manufactured in Brazil to the European subsidiaries. The availability of export swaps is completely dependent on the exports of Ace International to hard currency areas. These exports vary over time. The forecasts of these exports have been given by the European subsidiaries as in Table 4.6.

TABLE 4.6   Maximum Amounts of Export swaps

Month	Exports in Million Cruzeiros at Present Exchange Rates
1	731
2	1,750
3	1,620
4	1,000
5	1,120
6	1,580
7	1,490
8	900
9	700

Because of the chronic balance of payment problem, Brazil is vigorously promoting exports. This is why export swaps can be obtained at a relatively low cost. Export swaps are made available at the free market rate for cruzeiros. The hard currency deposit is still non-interest-bearing, but the cruzeiro cost has a reduced interest cost of 6%. Transaction costs of 2.5% are similar to the financial swap transaction costs. The total cost of an export swap consists, then, of the interest cost on the hard currency loan (6.8%), the interest cost on the cruzeiro loan (6%), and the transaction cost (2.5%).

Total cost is thus 15.3%. The variance of these costs is considered negligible. The export swap is valid for 3 months after the export invoice has been filed. There is not an optional early settlement clause as in the financial swap.

If ESW i equals the amount of the export swap contract concluded in month i, this variable is included in the model as follows:
Cost equation:

$$\text{CST } k = \cdots \text{(other terms)} \cdots + 0.01273 \text{ ESW } i, \qquad k = i, \ldots, i+2.$$

Cash equation:

$$\text{CSH } k = \cdots \text{(other terms)} \cdots + \text{ESW } k, \qquad k = 1, \ldots, 9;$$

$$\text{CSH}(k + 3) = \cdots \text{(other terms)} \cdots - 1.038 \text{ ESW } k.$$

Exposure equation:

$$\text{EXP } k = \cdots \text{(other terms)} \ldots - \text{ESW } i, \qquad k = i, \ldots, i + 2$$

Maximum constraint:

$$\text{ESW } k \leq \text{value of exports}, \qquad k = 1, \ldots, 9$$

(see Table 4.6).

4.9 Other Financing Sources

Some more specialized financing sources can be included in this presentation. American government funds abroad, acquired under Public Law 480, are an example of such sources. The Agency for International Development owns large funds in local currency originating from the export of American agricultural surplus. Loans from these funds are available at certain conditions, with a priority for the financing of fixed assets. In an operational use of the model, these sources should be included. But for this presentation, they would not add any new insight.

Use of blocked funds, or funds that became unconvertible for a variety of reasons, is another example of unconventional financing. These funds can sometimes be bought at a discount in hard currency. When this transaction is possible, blocked funds can constitute a very attractive financing source.

New types of financing procedures developed in recent years include also "link financing" and "arbi-loans."

All these transactions could be included in the model. To avoid undue complications in this presentation, we presume that none of these sources is possible in Brazil.

4.10 Bond Transactions

Cash in excess of the buffer stock and normal needs can and should be invested in short-term notes, treasury bonds, or prime-rate commercial paper. If excess cash is expected for longer periods, a stock portfolio is another alternative. Companies sometimes consider other uses of excess cash as a marketing promotion program. The treasurer of Ace International considers only investment in Brazilian treasury bonds at 12%.[14] These bonds are completely exposed to cruzeiro depreciation, but are otherwise considered as riskless. Transaction costs, buying and selling, amount to 1% and therefore reduce the net yield to 11%.

The Brazilian government has announced also a new type of hedging treasury bond. The bond has a maturity of 1 year and a yield of 12% per annum. The most important characteristic is that this bond is an unexposed asset because the face value is revalued every month at the free market exchange rate.[15] This hedging treasury bond will be available for 30 days at the beginning of the fourth month.[16] As a matter of policy, the company would not purchase more than 15 billion cruzeiros of this bond. All these bonds can be sold to generate cash in future periods. Define:

PTB i = purchase of normal treasury bonds in period i.

STB i = sale of normal treasury bonds in period i.

PHB 4 = purchase of hedging bond.

SHB $4 + j$ = sale of hedging bond in later periods.

The effects on the cash and exposure operations are obvious: A purchase causes a cash outflow, a sale causes an inflow, and the exposure is increased by the net amount of bonds held during the corresponding month. For example,

$$\text{CSH } 5 = \cdots \text{(other terms)} \cdots - \text{PTB } 5 + \text{STB } 5 + \text{SHB } 5;$$
$$\text{EXP } 5 = \cdots \text{(other terms)} \cdots + \text{PTB } 1 + \text{PTB } 2 + \text{PTB } 3$$
$$+ \text{PTB } 4 + \text{PTB } 5 - \text{STB } 2 - \text{STB } 3 - \text{STB } 4 - \text{STB } 5.$$

The constraint on maximum amount on bond sales is that sales in a given month remain smaller than bonds on hand (which equals previous purchases minus previous sales). For example,

$$\text{STB } 4 \leq \text{PTB } 1 + \text{PTB } 2 + \text{PTB } 3 + \text{PTB } 4 - \text{STB } 2 - \text{STB } 3$$
$$\text{SHB } 6 \leq \text{PHB } 4 - \text{SHB } 5$$
$$\text{PHB } 4 \leq 15 \text{ billion.}$$

14. Other investment possibilities could be easily included. At the limit, the Markowitz or Sharpe portfolio investment model could be set up as an integral part of the model.

15. This is a description, with some modifications, of the bond issued in Brazil in May–June 1966.

16. This bond behaves roughly as the purchase of some unrelated assets for hedging purposes. Companies buy steel sheets, raw materials, and so forth, unrelated to their business, when a devaluation threatens and no other hedge is available. They hope that a devaluation would not affect the dollar value of these assets. Such operations could be included in the model in the same fashion as the hedging treasury bond.

The bond transactions are the only profit-making operations in the Ace International case. The full profit equations can now be listed. But first it must be noted that the purchase of a treasury bond will yield an interest profit for all months following it. These interests are reduced by the sale of treaury bonds. For instance, PTB 2 will produce an interest inflow from months 2 to 9. If a sale of an equivalent amount of treasury bonds occurs in month 4, the interest flow is reduced by this amount from months 4 to 9. Only interest accrued in months 2 and 3 will remain in the equations. A similar technique is used to compute interest inflows of the hedging bond.

It is assumed that none of the bond transactions produces profits beyond the time horizon. In other words, all bonds are handled as if they were sold in the ninth month at the latest. The profits from bond transactions are:[17]

$$\text{PRT } 1 = 0.00916 \text{ PTB } 1$$

$$\text{PRT } 2 = 0.00916 \sum_{i=1}^{2} \text{PTB } i - 0.00916 \text{ STB } 2$$

$$\text{PRT } 3 = 0.00916 \sum_{i=1}^{3} \text{PTB } i - 0.00916 \sum_{i=2}^{3} \text{STB } i$$

$$\text{PRT } 4 = 0.00916 \sum_{i=1}^{4} \text{PTB } i + 0.00916 \text{ PHB } 4 - 0.00916 \sum_{i=2}^{4} \text{STB } i$$

$$\text{PRT } 5 = 0.00916 \sum_{i=1}^{5} \text{PTB } i + 0.00916 \text{ PHB } 4 - 0.00916 \sum_{i=2}^{5} \text{STB } i$$
$$- 0.00916 \text{ SHB } 5$$

$$\text{PRT } 6 = 0.00916 \sum_{i=1}^{6} \text{PTB } i + 0.00916 \text{ PHB } 4 - 0.00916 \sum_{i=2}^{6} \text{STB } i$$
$$- 0.00916 \sum_{i=5}^{6} \text{SHB,}$$

and so on.

4.11 Repatriation of Profits

Repatriation of profits can be considered from the point of view of the Brazilian subsidiary as an investment opportunity. One should "invest" in this opportunity when its subjective value is higher than all other alternative investment possibilities.

This immediately raises the question of how to determine the subjective value of a profit remittance. To the treasurer, the easiest way

17. The coefficients are $0.11/12 = 0.00916$.

to express the question is: "If a riskless unexposed government bond with an 8% yield is available, would you prefer to invest your earned surplus in this bond or repatriate the profits?" By varying the yield of this mythical bond, the subjective value to the treasurer of profit remittance can be evaluated.

There are some additional policy constraints. Ace International does not want to repatriate from Brazil more than 20% of net profit. On the other hand, the new regulations introduced by the United States to protect its balance of payment means, for Ace International in Brazil, a repatriation of at least 10% of net profits. Net profit, for the fiscal year, which ends with the seventh month of the planning period, is expected to be about 15 billion cruzeiros. Already 800 million cruzeiros have been repatriated in the 4 months immediately preceding the planning period. The Brazilian government does not restrict repatriation of this earned surplus, but the purchase of dollars is at the free market rate. As this exchange rate increases over time, the cost of remittances, expressed in cruzeiros, is increasing over time. See Table 4.7.

TABLE 4.7   Data on Repatriation of Profits

Month	Subjective Value of Profit Remittance	Cost of Remittance	Net Value	Variance
1	15%	2%	13%	0
2	15%	5%	10%	0.0004
3	15%	10%	5%	0.0009
4	20%	14%	6%	0.001
5	20%	18%	2%	0.0012
6	30%	24%	8%	0.0015
7	35%	28%	7%	0.002
8	10%	30%	−20%	0.0025
9	10%	36%	−26%	0.003

The subjective value of a profit remittance increases from the fourth to the seventh month, because the financial statement to the stockholders is published in the seventh month. The performance of the Brazilian operation is judged, among others, by these profit remittances. Having the remittances effectuated before this publication is of increasing value to the treasurer. For the same reason, remittances in the eighth and ninth month are of little value to him.

The cost of the remittance in the first month is simply the transaction cost of about 2%. But as dollars become more and more expensive at the free market rate, this cost increases rapidly. The variance of these costs is the variance on the free market rate, which is high.

Remember that there are really two ways by which we can repatriate profits: The first one has just been presented; and the second one uses the possibility of forward exchange remittances. The forward-exchange contracts are used to buy now the right to remit profits at a fixed rate in later periods. This second technique is less risky but is subject to government control, as was explained earlier.

Let REP i equal the repatriation of profits in period i, then the constraint of maximum repatriation of profits is

$$\sum_{i=1}^{7} \text{REP } i + \sum_{i=3}^{4} \text{FTA } i + \sum_{i=3}^{4} \text{FFA } i + \sum_{i=5}^{6} \text{FTB } i + \sum_{i=5}^{6} \text{FFB } i$$
$$\leq 2.2 \text{ billion cruzeiros.}[18]$$

The minimal constraint on profit repatriation is

$$\sum_{i=1}^{7} \text{REP } i + \sum_{i=3}^{4} \text{FTA } i + \sum_{i=3}^{4} \text{FFA } i + \sum_{i=5}^{6} \text{FTB } i + \sum_{i=5}^{6} \text{FFB } i$$
$$\geq 700,000,000 \text{ cruzeiros.}[19]$$

The other equations where the REP i variables appear are cash constraints and the objective function.

Cash constraint:

$$\text{CSH } 1 = \cdots \text{(other terms)} \cdots - \text{REP } i.$$

Objective function:

$$\text{maximize } Z = \cdots \text{(other terms)} \cdots + 0.13 \text{ REP } 1 + 0.1 \text{ REP } 2$$
$$+ 0.05 \text{ REP } 3 \cdots - 0.0004 (\text{REP } 2)^2 - 0.0009 (\text{REP } 3)^2 \cdots$$

4.12 Inventory Hedging

Earlier the exposure of inventories was defined, and how it can be measured was explained (Section 4.3.4). It was shown that some products could be considered unexposed or even negatively exposed under certain circumstances. It is therefore not astonishing that inventories are sometimes used as hedges.

By accumulating excess inventories of unexposed products, a company can reduce its excess cash position before the devaluation.

18. That is, 2.2 billion = (0.2 × 15 billion) − 800 million (already remitted).
19. That is, 700 million = (0.1 × 15 billion) − 800 million.

Just before a devaluation, companies sometimes even buy products unrelated to their business when no other hedging possibilities are available (products such as gold, steel plates, copper wire, industrial diamonds are examples). This latter — and desperate — case is not considered in this model.

What is the cost of inventory hedging? If the product is related to the company's business, an accumulation of raw materials has only storage costs as incremental costs to the normal operations without hedging. The cost of hedging is, therefore, simply the cost of placing an order larger than the optimal lot order size.

This raises the often incorrectly solved problem of determining the optimal lot order under conditions of hyperinflation and devaluation.[20] The classical inventory models underevaluate very strongly the optimal order size, by neglecting the future price increases of the product purchased.

4.12.1   A Digression On Optimal Lot Order Size under Inflation

The classical inventory models assume a constant purchase price. Therefore, the economic order sizes determined from these models are completely unreliable under conditions in which prices change because of devaluation and inflation.

The key formula is the determination of economic order sizes, since most other parameters can be derived from this value.[21] The simplified classical model for inventory control will be compared with two other formulas, one for constant price increases, and another for step price increases. The models assume no safety stock, no back ordering, and a deterministic and regular sales flow.

These assumptions are, of course, limiting the operational use of these formulas. In making them, the hope is simply to demonstrate the importance of price changes in inventory control. Operational models can be derived from the simplified cases given here.

(a) CLASSICAL INVENTORY MODEL.   As a reference point, the classical

20. An anecdote: a large international company sent a team of operations research specialists to Argentina to reorganize the inventory system of the company's subsidiary. They neglected the inflation factor in the determination of optimal lot sizes. A year later, when someone in the headquarters noticed the error, an inquiry was made on the Argentina inventory control. The purchase officer in Argentina had never applied the recommended lot sizes but had added an intuitive amount to the order sizes to take into account expected price raises.

21. If X is the optimal economic order size, order frequency $= f =$ annual sales$/X$; storage time $= t = X/$annual sales; average inventory level $=$ safety stock $+ X/2$.

formula for optimal lot order sizes is used:

$$X_1 = \sqrt{\frac{2UK}{P(i+j)}}$$

where

X = optimal order size (in number of items, weights, etc.),
U = annual sales (units/year),
K = fixed order costs, independent of order size ($/unit),
P = price per unit ordered,
  i = interest rate charged to average capital tied up in inventory (%/year),
  j = coefficient to charge to an order the corresponding annual inventory costs (%/year).

(b) MODEL FOR STEADY PRICE INCREASES.[22]   When the cost of a unit increases with a regular rate a, the economic order quantity is

$$X_2 = \sqrt{\frac{2U(K+F)}{P[r - 2a + (1+s)i]}}$$

where

F = fixed cost to maintain the inventory ($/year),

a = percent of steady increase,

$$r = \frac{k_1}{P}$$

where k_1 equals the inventory cost varying with quantities and storage time (that is, cleaning, corrosion prevention, and so forth);

$$s = \frac{k_2}{P}$$

where k_2 equals the inventory cost depending on order size but not on storage time (that is, cost of putting items in and out of store).
This formula would apply to items whose cost is pegged to a regularly increasing index.

(c) MODEL FOR STEP PRICE INCREASES.   When a step price increase of

22. The formulas of steady price increases and step increases come from L. Pack, *Optimale Bestellmenge und Optimale Lossgröbe — Zu einigen Problemen ihrer Ermittlung*, Wiesbaden, 1964. Demonstrations of the formulas are given in this work.

$b\%$ is expected before the next purchase, a larger quantity should be ordered to take advantage of the lower cost at the present purchase.

$$X_3 = \sqrt{\frac{2U(K + F)}{P[i(1 + s)(1 + b) + wb + r]} + \frac{Ub}{i(1 + s)(1 + b) + wb + r}}$$

where

  b = percent increase in one step,

  w = inventory losses (units/year).

(d) COMPARISON OF THE THREE MODELS. To demonstrate the changes in optimal inventory policies when price changes are taken into account, all three models were simulated. The TROLL system at the time-sharing facility at M.I.T. was used for these simulations.

For each level of price increase the 3 formulas (a, b, and c) are solved. All parameters common to all 3 formulas are identical. The parameters appearing only in one of the formulas were determined to give identical lot order sizes when the price increase is zero percent. The classical formula always gives the same quantity as an optimal order size, whatever the price increase (see Figure 4.8).

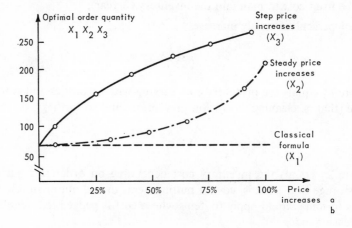

FIGURE 4.8   Comparison of Three Inventory Models

The steady price increase formula deviates only marginally from the classical formula at a low rate of price change (10% larger optimal lot order size for a 25% price increase per year). The deviation becomes very large at higher inflation levels (250% larger order size for a 100% price increase per annum).

The step price increases have a drastic effect on optimal lot order sizes, even at low levels of price hikes (120% increase for only a 25% price hike).

In summary, price increases, especially in the form of discrete steps, have a dramatic impact on inventory policy. The increases in inventory levels suggested by these formulas are dictated only by inventory policy. No financial consideration — specifically, no hedging — has been involved up to this point.

4.12.2 *Hedging with Inventories*

Suppose that the company is working exactly at optimal inventory levels, adjusted for expected price increases. Suppose also that an excess cash position has been developing, and a devaluation is ahead. The government clamped down exchange controls to avoid currency outflows. No forward-exchange contracts are available, and all other hedging means are outrageously expensive.

The only solution left to reduce the exposure is to accumulate inventories of nonexposed products, even beyond the optimal inventory level. The cost of going beyond the optimal inventory level is the cost of this type of hedging.

Ace International uses as raw materials several products that can be considered as reasonably unexposed. The ability to accumulate large stocks of such goods is limited by the warehouse capacities of the company. At all times, the warehouse has an unused capacity for 300 million cruzeiros of unexposed products. The average cost of going beyond optimal inventory levels is estimated at 10% up to full capacity of the warehouse.

Going beyond the 300 million cruzeiros excess inventory requires leasing of storage space. The cost of the lease, the additional transportation expense from the leased warehouses to the production facilities, additional insurances, and so forth brings the total cost to 35%. Another 500 million cruzeiros of goods can be stored at that price.[23]

The variances of these costs are low for the excess inventory accumulated in the warehouses of the company (variance = 0.0004). The cost on the leased storage space is fairly unpredictable and is therefore taxed with a higher variance (0.0015). Define:

EIW i = excess inventory in the company's warehouses purchased during month i;

EIL i = excess inventory in leased storage space purchased during month i;

23. More involved cost constraints can easily be included by multiplying the number of variables.

Excess inventory means inventories accumulated beyond the optimal level determined in Section 4.12.1. The variables just defined will appear in the following equations:
Objective function:

maximize $Z = \cdots$ (other terms) $\cdots$

$$-0.0004 \sum_{i=1}^{9} (\text{EIW } i)^2 - 0.0015 \sum_{i-1}^{9} (\text{EIL } i)^2$$

Cost equation:

$$\text{CST } k = 0.00839 \sum_{i=1}^{k} \text{EIW } i + 0.0297 \sum_{i=1}^{k} \text{EIL } i \qquad k = 1, \ldots, 9.$$

Cash constraint:

$$\text{CSH } k = \cdots \text{(other terms)} \cdots - \text{EIW } k - \text{EIL } k$$

Maximum constraints:

$$\sum_{k=1}^{9} \text{EIW } k \le 300 \text{ million cruzeiros}$$

$$\sum_{k=1}^{9} \text{EIL } k \le 500 \text{ million cruzeiros}$$

Notice that payment and receipt of inventories were assumed to occur in the same month. A credit purchase, with payment due one month later, would shift the variable into the cash constraint of the month $(k + 1)$.

4.13   Other Constraints
A large number of other types of constraints could be made integral parts of the model. The loan covenants or restrictions on bond indenture on any specific loan or bond contract is one example. Balance sheet covenants such as ratios of working capital to fixed assets, maximum on dividends payments, compensating balances, can easily be included.[24]

Another type of constraint is company policy decisions. Some financial constraints are decided by company policy, like the quick ratio.[25]

24. J. Van Horne, "A linear programming approach to evaluating restrictions under bond indenture or loan agreement," *Journal of Finance and Quantitative Analysis* vol. 1, (June 1966), pp. 68–83.

25. Yair Orgler: "An Unequal-Period Model for Cash Management by Business Firms," unpublished manuscript presented at TIMS/ORSA joint meeting, San Francisco, May 1968.

All these constraints could easily be handled by the model but do not add any additional insight into the technique. They have, therefore, not been considered in the Ace International case.

The Ace International case is now complete. The question remains: What is the solution to the problem that was presented? What are the transactions the treasurer should engage in, in what amounts, and when? This is the topic of the next chapter.

5

Ace International Case: The Solution

The case study developed in Chapter 4 has been solved. Only 3 solutions will be analyzed in detail: a very conservative strategy ($L = 0.2$); an intermediary strategy ($L = 200$); and a solution close to the extreme cost minimization ($L = 6,052$). The strategies are selected to show 3 typical solutions from the model rather than a set of 3 choices that would be meaningful to a company treasurer in real life. Even the "high-risk" solutions in this specific problem have a reasonably low variance. Therefore, in the business world, only the solutions at the high-risk end of the spectrum would be of practical interest.

5.1 Overview of the Three Strategies

In this section, short overviews of the 3 solutions are displayed simultaneously, showing how the 3 strategies relate to one another. A more detailed study of all the relevant decision variables follows: (Only the variables that are nonzero in at least 1 of the 3 strategies studied are given.)

COST = total expected costs (financing and hedging).
PROF = total expected profit (treasury bond operations).
CST k = costs incurred in month k (see details in Section 4.3.1).
PRT k = profits realized in month k (see details in Section 4.3.1).
EXP k = net resulting exposure in month k (see Section 4.3.3).
BLA k = amount of local bank loan, type A, accepted in month k (see Section 4.5.1).
BLB k = same, type B.
BLC k = same, type C.
BLD k = same, type D.
PLA 1 = amount of private loan A of month 1 (see Section 4.5.2).
PLB 4 = amount of private loan B of month 4 (see Section 4.5.2).
PLC 7 = amount of private loan C of month 7 (see Section 4.5.2).

S\$L k = amount of straight dollar loan imported in month k (see Section 4.6).

FFA 4 = amount of forward-exchange contract taken in month 4, corresponding to the nonturnaround SUMOC 289 loan A (see Section 4.7).

FTB 5 = amount of forward-exchange contract taken in month 5, corresponding to the turnaround SUMOC loan B (see Section 4.7).

FSW 2 = amount of financial swap available in month 2 (see Section 4.8).

ESW k = amount of export swap available accepted in month k (see Section 4.8).

SSW 8 = settlement of financial swap in month 8 (see Section 4.8).

PTB k = purchase of treasury bonds in month k.

STB k = sale of treasury bonds in month k.

PHB 4 = purchase of hedging bonds available in month 4.

SHB k = sale of hedging bonds in month k.

REP k = repatriation of profits in month k.

EIW k = excess inventory purchases in month k, stored in own warehouses.

EIL k = excess inventory purchases in month k, stored in leased warehouses.

Table 5.1 displays the values of the variables for the 3 selected strategies and should be referred to every time a variable in one of the strategies is discussed. The low-risk strategy has an expected cost total of 5,014 million cruzeiros and a variance of 8,070. At the other extreme, the high-risk strategy is characterized by an expected cost of 4,323 million cruzeiros and a variance of 27,488.

The 3 strategies studied are relatively close to one another. Total expected costs at both ends of the spectrum differ only by 14%, but the details of the 3 solutions are more varied than this resultant measure would lead us to suppose.

5.2   The Low-Risk, High-Cost Strategy

This solution, the low-risk, high-cost strategy ($L = 0.2$), is studied merely for academic interest. The variance of this strategy is low ($V = 8,070$), while the expected cost is comparatively high (in millions of cruzeiros, $E = 5,014$). No company would be so risk averse as to sacrifice to such an extent the minimization of expected costs. The very heavy weight given to variance reduction sometimes makes this solution look foolish. For example, some cheaper local loans are not used to capacity, while more expensive local loans are tapped.

TABLE 5.1 Values of Variables in the Three Selected Strategies* in Millions of Cruzeiros at Present Exchange Rates

	A	B	C
Parameter L	0.2	200	6,052
Expected Cost E	5,014	4,338	4,323
Variance V	8,070	19,808	27,488
COST	5,345	4,881	4,864
PROF	346	336	336
CST 1	54	76	82
CST 2	120	124	127
CST 3	254	227	229
CST 4	455	416	413
CST 5	517	451	440
CST 6	513	447	441
CST 7	641	629	598
CST 8	688	718	711
CST 9	803	762	754
CST *	1,296	1,027	1,064
PRT 1	11	21	23
PRT 3	23	13	13
PRT 4	128	114	114
PFT 5	98	92	89
PRT 6	42	36	36
PRT 7	36	36	36
PRT 8	4	19	21
EXP 1	3,258	4,414	4,414
EXP 5	14	527	859
EXP 7	28		
EXP 9	88		
BLA 1	234		
BLA 2	773	497	289
BLA 3	600	600	600
BLA 4	900	900	900
BLA 5	700	700	700
BLA 6	700	367	700
BLA 7	600	600	600
BLA 8	500	500	500
BLA 9	500	500	500
BLB 1	37		
BLB 2	125		
BLB 3	351		
BLB 4	424	1,700	1,700
BLB 5	377	1,700	1,159
BLB 6	298		
BLB 7	1,400	1,400	1,400
BLB 8	1,400	1,400	1,400

TABLE 5.1—*Continued*

	A	B	C
BLB 9	1,400	1,400	1,400
BLC 1	25		
BLC 2	116		
BLC 3	334		
BLC 4	438	337	
BLC 5	568		
BLC 6	289		
BLC 7	2,139	5,200	5,200
BLC 8	1,819	4,267	5,200
BLC 9	1,815	675	839
BLD 1	14		
BLD 2	106		
BLD 3	330		
BLD 4	453		
BLD 5	558		
BLD 6	280		
BLD 7	2,130	1,467	370
BLD 8	1,810		
BLD 9	1,805		
PLA 1	83	770	1,260
PLB 4	120	225	280
PLC 7	40	150	1,400
S$L 1	4,008	6,164	6,192
S$L 3	7,670	7,670	7,670
S$L 4	13,995	11,713	11,693
FFA 4	700		
FTB 5	1,416		
FSW 2	1,000	1,000	1,000
SSW 8	1,000	1,000	1,000
ESW 1	731	282	
ESW 2	1,750	1,750	1,750
ESW 3	1,620	1,620	1,620
ESW 4	1,000	1,000	1,000
ESW 5	1,120	1,120	1,120
ESW 6	1,580	1,580	1,580
ESW 7	1,490	1,490	1,490
ESW 8	900	900	900
ESW 9	700	700	700
PTB 1	1,285	2,367	2,575
PTB 3	2,546	1,520	1,520
PTB 6	687		
PTB 8	337	2,172	2,340
STB 2	1,285	2,367	2,575
STB 4	2,546	1,520	1,520
STB 7	687		
STB 9	337	2,172	2,340

TABLE 5.1—*Concluded*

	A	B	C
PHB 4	14,008	12,463	12,453
SHB 5	3,300	2,351	2,672
SHB 6	6,733	6,116	5,784
SHB 8	3,797	3,994	3,978
SHB 9	186		18
REP 1		1,000	1,027
REP 7	83	1,200	1,172
EIW 2	243		
EIW 7	56		
EIL 7	173		

* Only the variables that are nonzero in at least 1 of the 3 strategies are listed.

The strategies will be studied by groups of variables: first, the decision variables (bank loans, forward-exchange contracts, swaps, and so forth), and then the resulting variables (costs and exposures).

A first group of decision variables relates to local loans. The bank loans, type *A*, are the cheapest local loans available (see Section 4.5). Most of them are used to capacity (BLA 3 to BLA 9). The type *B* bank loans are used to capacity in only the 3 last months, when the probability of a large devaluation is highest, making local financing more attractive. Smaller amounts of the very expensive local loans *C* and *D* are also used. Finally, the private loans are practically negligible in this strategy (in millions of cruzeiros, PLA 1 = 83; PLB 4 = 120; PLC 7 = 40),[1] because their high variance makes them undesirable.

The straight dollar financing is the second group of decision variables. This source of funds is cheaper than local financing but does not reduce the net exposure. The basic cash requirements of the first month, when no devaluation is possible, are satisfied with straight dollar loans (S$L 1 = 4,008 millions of cruzeiros). The only other 2 months in which dollar loans are imported are months 3 and 4. During month 3, there is a very heavy basic cash requirement and a comparatively low basic exposure (see Sections 4.3.2 and 4.3.3); Therefore, the dollar loan is advisable. The very large dollar loan of month 4 (S$L 4 = 13,995 millions of cruzeiros) is used to purchase the treasury hedging bond that is available only during that month. As this hedging bond is not

1. The variables are expressed in millions of cruzeiros at present exchange rates.

an exposed asset, again dollar financing is recommended. In summary, because of the high devaluation probabilities in most of the months, local financing is preferred. It is only when the devaluation probability is zero, or when the cash required does not increase the net exposure, that dollar financing is suggested.

The next variable group relates to the forward-exchange contracts. Only 2 forward-exchange contracts are available (see Section 4.7). Forward-exchange contract A is used to capacity, and without a turn-about operation (FFA $4 = 700$ millions of cruzeiros). The option is executed in month 4. Recall that a forward-exchange contract without turnabout is a financing source (see Section 4.7). The reason for this forward-exchange contract is to bring in dollars for investment in the hedging bond and, in addition, to allow for some coverage in the 3 following months. The forward-exchange contract B, in contrast, is turned around, and the option is executed in month 5 (FTB $5 = 1,416$ million cruzeiros). This is a pure hedging operation aimed at the reduction of the exposure in months 5 to 8.

All of the group of variables representing the swap transactions are taken to capacity (see Section 4.8). The financial swap available in month 2 is accepted. The option to settle occurs at the latest possible moment (FSW $2 = 1,000$ and SSW $8 = 1,000$ millions of cruzeiros). All the export swaps are accepted also, as they represent a comparatively cheap source of local financing.

The next group of decision variables refers to all the treasury bond transactions (see Section 4.10). The normal treasury bond transactions are used to invest idle cash available in a period for use in later periods. For instance, heavy cash requirement is due in month 7, and cheap local loans are exhausted in that month. It pays to raise money in earlier periods — for example, in month 6 where cheaper money is still available — and invest it in normal treasury bills. These bills are sold in month 7 to generate some additional cash. These bond transactions can therefore be considered as a device to even out cash fluctuations (see Figure 5.1).

The hedging bond operations perform fundamentally the same task, but the hedging bond has the additional advantage of being a non-exposed asset. Therefore, cheaper U.S. dollars are imported to purchase them. The hedging bonds are liquidated bit by bit in later periods to cover cash needs (Figure 5.2). In fact, 14 billion cruzeiros of hedging bonds are purchased in month 4. This creates a heavy cash drain in this month, which explains why the largest sale of normal treasury bonds occurs at that time (see Figure 5.1). These hedging bonds are used as

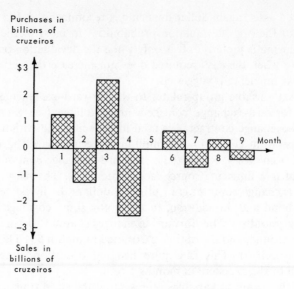

FIGURE 5.1   Normal Treasury Bond Transactions

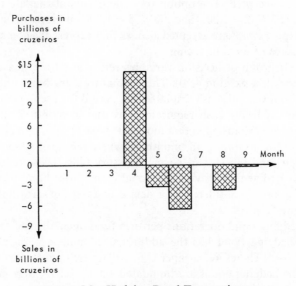

FIGURE 5.2   Hedging Bond Transactions

a financing source in months 5, 6, and 8, and, to a limited extent, in month 9.

The bond transactions are the only ones in the Ace International case that would create a profit. The normal treasury bonds purchased in month 1, and immediately sold in month 2, yield a profit of 11 million cruzeiros (PRT $1 = 11$). Similarly, the profits generated in month 3 are from normal treasury bonds (PRT $3 = 23$). The balance of the profits relate mostly to hedging bond transactions. These profits level off as the hedging bonds are sold (PRT $4 = 128$ to PRT $8 = 4$). Total profits represent 346 million cruzeiros (PROF $= 346$).

Repatriations of profits are only minor in this strategy. Since the repayments of forward-exchange contracts are considered to be repatriations of profits, only a small formal repatriation of profits is required (see Section 4.11). This repatriation is effectuated at the time when it has the highest subjective value to the treasurer, that is, in month 7 (REP $7 = 83$). This is just before the yearly report of Brazilian operations (see Section 4.11 for details).

Finally, hedging with inventories is also performed. Excess inventories in the company's own warehouses are purchased to capacity in 2 installments: in months 2 and 7 (EIW $2 = 243$ and EIW $7 = 56$). As the exposure in month 7 is still positive and no other kind of hedging is available, some excess inventories to be stored in leased warehouses are also recommended (EIL $7 = 173$).

The net exposure resulting from this strategy is extremely high in only the first month (EXP $1 = 3,258$). No efforts to reduce this exposure have been made because the probability of a devaluation was considered zero (see Sections 4.2 and 4.3.3). This explains why local financing in the first month was low, even for the cheapest bank loans. Straight dollar loans were used instead.

The exposure in the remaining months is typically either small or zero. In month 5, when the probability of a devaluation is comparatively low, only 14 million cruzeiros are exposed (EXP $5 = 14$). Some additional and relatively cheap hedging was available (for example, BLB 5) but was not judged necessary. The expected devaluation loss is too small to justify coverage. In months 7 and 9, the scarcity of cheap hedging possibilities explains the remaining net exposure (EXP $7 = 28$ and EXP $9 = 88$). These months also had a very high basic net exposure (Section 4.3.3).

The last group of variables remaining to be discussed is the resulting financing and hedging costs. The monthly costs are increasing gradually from 54 million cruzeiros in month 1 to 1,296 million cruzeiros beyond the time horizon. Total costs represent 5,345 million cruzeiros (COST $= 5,345$). Compared to the other strategies, in the first months costs are low but are very high in later periods. Therefore, this strategy is very conservative for two reasons: It is a low-risk strategy because of the heavy emphasis on the reduction of the variance; also it is a low-risk strategy because only small costs are incurred in the first months. If we implement the recommendations of the first month and if it later develops that our estimates of subsequent periods are extremely bad, only relatively small expenses will have been incurred up to that time (CST 1 = 54 in this strategy, while in the high-risk strategy it is CST 1 = 82).

In summary, the described strategy is typically an extreme risk-averting solution. Total costs are substantial, but their variance is low.

5.3 The Intermediary Strategy

In this intermediary strategy ($L = 200$), the anomalies as a result of extreme risk aversion disappear. This solution follows the same pattern as that in the low-risk, high-cost solution.

The local bank loans are not used at all in the first month, and only the cheapest local loans (type A) are tapped in months 2, 3 and 6. The heaviest use of the local market occurs in month 7, where the bank loans A, B, and C are all used to capacity; even some of the most expensive local loan is tapped (BLD 7 = 1,467). The other heavy months use only the type B loans (BLB 4 = BLB 5 = 1,700 and BLB 7 = BLB 8 = BLB 9 = 1,400). Every time a cheaper bank loan is exhausted, the more expensive ones are used to complete the coverage of the local financing needs.

The private loans, which have a high variance, are used more extensively than they were previously in the conservative solution, but not yet to capacity (PLA 1 = 770, PLB 4 = 225, and PLC 7 = 150).

The straight dollar loans are now used to finance all cash requirements of the first month. The other dollar loans perform the same task as they did previously. Specifically in month 3, some dollars are imported because cash requirements are higher than the net exposure. The purchase of the hedging bond in month 4 is, again, almost exclusively financed with dollars.

Very few changes occur in the swap transactions. The only difference is a lower use of the export swaps in month 1. The principle of replacing local and expensive funds by imported dollars is pushed further in this case than in the previous low-risk, high-cost strategy.

The bond transactions perform basically the same task as previously, although the amounts and timing are different.

Notice that in the present intermediary strategy no forward-exchange contracts are accepted. The repatriation of profits has, therefore, to be performed in the form of official transfers (see Section 4.11). The maximum possible amount is repatriated in 2 installments (REP 1 =

1,000 and REP 7 = 1,200). The repatriatation in month 1 is carried out when the costs of transfer are the lowest. The second repatriation, in month 7, is accomplished when the subjective value of repatriation is at its highest. No inventory hedging is performed in this strategy.

The net exposure resulting from this intermediary strategy is quite different from the one in the low-risk, high-cost solution. The net exposure of month 1, when the probability of a devaluation is nil, is now very high (EXP 1 = 4,414). This increase is the result of the replacement of virtually all local financing by dollar loans along with a higher amount of normal treasury bond purchased during month 1. The only other month in which the net exposure is not zero is month 5 (EXP 5 = 527). The probability and the possible amount of a devaluation are fairly low at month 5 (see Section 4.2). Nonetheless, this strategy is riskier than the low-risk, high-cost one, because the net exposure is higher.

The costs involved in the intermediary strategy are lower than those of the previous one (COST = 4,881). Profits on bond transactions are also reduced but by only a very small amount compared to the cost reductions (PROF = 336). Also, the timing of the cost outlays is different. More costs are incurred in the first months and less toward the end.

The net expected cost is lower, but the variance increases to 19,808. The cost reductions are, therefore, compensated by a serious increase in the variance of the total strategy.

5.4 The High-Risk, Low-Cost Strategy

The high-risk, low-cost strategy ($L = 6,052$) is not dramatically different from the intermediary strategy. Total expected costs are reduced by only 15 million cruzeiros, which represents less than 0.5%. The increase in the variance is much larger: It is now 27,488. In most variables, only minor changes occur. For instance, most bank loans are identical with those in the intermediary solution. BLA 2 and BLB 5 are a little smaller, while BLA 6, BLB 8, and BLB 9 are higher. One variable (BLC 4) drops out of the solution. The private loans are used much more extensively, some of them even being taken to capacity.

However, very little change occurs in the dollar financing. The only difference in the swap transactions is that ESW 1 disappears from the solution vector. Also, only minor changes are apparent in the other transactions (treasury bonds and repatriations of profits). The resulting exposure in month 1 is identical to that of the intermediary case, but the exposure of month 5 has increased substantially (EXP 5 = 859).

The profits on the treasury bonds amount to the same in both cases, but the costs of hedging and financing have been reduced. The timing of these costs is still more concentrated in the beginning periods than in the 2 previous strategies.

5.5   Conclusion of the Ace International Case

Three different strategies were briefly described as solutions for the Ace International problem. The rationale on which each of these solutions is based was analyzed.

The A ce International case was not presented as an example of the realistic use of the model: A large variety of transactions were analyzed and incorporated into the model so that one example might indicate the manner in which the model handles real-life transactions and constraints. A real problem has typically a smaller variety of variables but a larger number of variables in each variety.

The Ace International case is only a starting point. A number of assumptions were made that were not analyzed in depth. Some limitations imposed on the case involve key factors, which should be taken into account — as, for example, international taxation or correlation between variables.

Chapters 6 and 7 review these assumptions and limitations with more care than previously. It is only after this study of the key assumptions and limitations is presented that an operationally useful model can be constructed.

6
Refinements of the Ace
International Case

Some of the limitations and simplifying assumptions of the Ace International case are eliminated in this chapter. For example, Chapters 4 and 5 neglected all correlations between business risks, as well as the effects of taxation. These topics are now treated. The underlying assumptions of the correlation system of devaluation data are also discussed in more depth. To make the model more flexible for managerial use, some further options are added: changing profit and cost preferences over time as well as choosing among mutually exclusive and contingent decisions. These topics were not discussed earlier because they would have obscured the main theme of the argument. It was more important to present an overall view of the model than the intricacies of these comparatively minor points.

6.1. Correlations Between Devaluation Data
Up to this point in the Ace International case, all the correlations between decision variables were neglected. The only correlations taken into account were the ones between devaluation estimates of the successive months, and even these correlations were simplistic: a perfect positive correlation for devaluation amounts, and a decreasing positive correlation of probabilities over time (see Section 4.2). These assumptions are now discussed in depth.

6.1.1 *Correlations of Devaluation Amounts*
Recall that a positive correlation measures the tendency of two random variables to move in the same direction. If the time units are short, a very high positive correlation for devaluation amounts over time is a fairly reasonable assumption. For example, it is logical that the amount by which a currency would depreciate in January would be strongly

related to the amount of a possible devaluation in February. There was a consensus that the pound sterling would devalue by 10% to 15% during the winter of 1967–1968. The problem was in the timing. The assumption of a positive correlation of devaluation amounts reflects the following fact: If in September 1967, the pound sterling threatened to depreciate by an amount on the high side of the 10% to 15% range, the possible devaluation in October 1967 would also be on the high side of this range.

If the time units of a multitemporal model are longer periods — for example, years — the high positive correlation is not necessarily valid. If a parity-modification possibility in January 1966 is in fact on the high side of a given range, it has perhaps no relationship with the position of the devaluation amount of another range in January 1967. In a year's time, a government can apply deflationary policies that could completely change the devaluation outlook. Therefore, the size of the time units is a critical ingredient in estimating the correlations of the devaluation amounts.

Because the Ace International case has monthly time units, it is clear the perfect positive correlation of devaluation amount random variables is a fair assumption.

6.1.2 Correlations of Devaluation Probabilities

Devaluation amounts do not change drastically in short time periods. In contrast, strong fluctuations in devaluation probabilities exist, sometimes on a daily basis. The simplistic treatment of correlations of devaluation probabilities presented in the Ace International case is, therefore, more suspect than the treatment of the amounts. The correlation of the probability of devaluation for any given month with the one immediately following it was assumed to be 0.75. The correlation with the estimate of 2 months later was 0.50, and that of 3 months later was 0.25. All other correlations were assumed negligible.

The correlation matrix used in the Ace International case is presented in Table 6.1. The values of the correlations $\tilde{d}_k\ \tilde{d}_m$ are listed for each month's indices k and m.

Are the implicit assumptions represented in this matrix valid? The correlation matrix implies a set of *error waves* in the system (see Figure 6.1).

If the devaluation probability of the first month is higher than expected, the same tendency is assumed for the second month (because the correlation $\tilde{d}_1\ \tilde{d}_2 = 0.75$). This second month probability in turn affects the devaluation probability of the third month (because the correlation $\tilde{d}_2\ \tilde{d}_3 = 0.75$), and the third month probability has an

TABLE 6.1 Correlation Matrix of Devaluation Data*

m	k							
	1	2	3	4	5	6	7	8
1								
2	0.75							
3	0.50	0.75						
4	0.25	0.50	0.75					
5		0.25	0.50	0.75				
6			0.25	0.50	0.75			
7				0.25	0.50	0.75		
8					0.50	0.75	0.75	
9						0.25	0.50	0.75

* Only the lower half of the matrix is given, an amount sufficient to define a symmetric matrix.

impact on the fourth month, and so forth. This first error wave can be visualized as a dampened oscillation over time. The oscillation is dampened because the correlation coefficient is smaller than 1. Another set of even more dampened oscillations (correlation = 0.50) is communicated by the correlations between $\tilde{d}_1 \tilde{d}_3$, and $\tilde{d}_2 \tilde{d}_4$, and so on. Finally, a third wave is generated by the correlations between $\tilde{d}_1 \tilde{d}_4$, $\tilde{d}_2 \tilde{d}_5$, and so forth. All these oscillations are superimposed on one another.

Remember that all these oscillations are generated by a deviation from the expected value of the devaluation probability only in the first month. A similar process can start in the second month, for example; and the new set of waves generated by deviations in the second month are superimposed on the first set. This process could also start in subsequent periods. The whole system is affected by these cumulative perturbations over time.

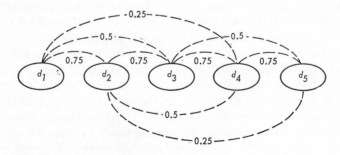

FIGURE 6.1 Correlation System of Devaluation Data

It is useful now to go back to Figure 4.1 and to consider the comments of the Brazilian economist. (See Section 4.2.) What does this
described cumulative effect of the set of error waves represent physically
in terms of the Brazilian devaluation outlook? A graphical representation is given in Figure 6.2.

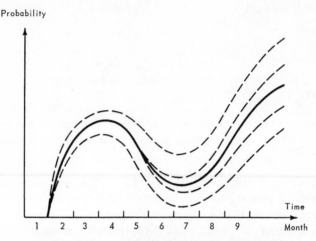

FIGURE 6.2   Effect of Positive Probability Correlations

A relatively small deviation from the expected probability in the
beginning is transmitted through the system with increasing amplitude.
This would be true on the upper side as well as on the lower one. This
phenomenon can appear anywhere in the system. Figure 6.2 describes
one such deviation starting in the second month and another one in the
fourth month.

In what circumstances is this pattern a valid assumption? Two factors must be taken into account: the size of the time units and the
number of independent devaluation possibilities expected in the total
time horizon. The first factor, explained in the previous paragraph, is
straightforward. If the time units are years, the probabilities of a devaluation often have little relationship with one another. In very unstable
economies, or in times of an international monetary crisis, not even
monthly probabilities could be at all correlated. Because of these
circumstances, among other reasons, an unequally divided time-horizon
model is developed in Chapter 7. In less extreme cases, probabilities
of devaluations fluctuate over time, and some patterns can be discerned.
For example, when devaluations are the result of slow inflationary
pressures or structural deficiencies, years of cumulative small crises
may occur before the authorities are forced to readjust the parity of
a currency. Probabilities of devaluations obviously have a trend in

these circumstances. The French devaluations during the interwar period are examples in point: Budget deficits were the most obvious causes of inflation; and as these deficits accumulated, the probability of a foreign exchange crisis increased proportionately.[1] Today accumulation of foreign debt servicing in developing nations, especially in Africa, plays a similar role.[2]

When trends in devaluation probabilities exist, very often a positive correlation system such as the one used in the Ace International case study is a valid assumption. What Figure 6.1 would mean conceptually is that an error in the probability estimation in any month creates a tendency to revise the probabilities of all later months in the same direction, with an increasing amplitude.

The degree of the increase in the amplitude over time as a feature of the model is entirely under the control of the manager. By changing the values of the correlation coefficients, the error waves are weakened or strengthened at will. In practical use, however, these correlations can be fixed according to the length of the time units of the model and the instability of the economy. Only when one of those factors changes drastically should a revision be imperative.

Up to now, one important remark of the Brazilian economist of Ace International was overlooked. He expects *either* a mild devaluation from month 2 to 5, *or* a larger one toward the end of the planning period. He does not expect both devaluations to occur but cannot decide at this time which one will actually materialize. This statement implies that, if the probability of a devaluation turns out to be higher than expected for the first devaluation, logically the probability of the second should be lower, and vice versa. Figure 6.3 depicts this assumption. To describe this pattern mathematically, it is necessary to introduce negative error waves. In terms of the correlation coefficients, it suffices to change the signs of the terms crossing the separation line of the 2 potential devaluations. The resulting correlation matrix is given in Table 6.2.

If the Brazilian economist believes very strongly that those two devaluation possibilities tend to be mutually exclusive, a more powerful matrix can be prepared. In Table 6.3, the slightest increase in the probability of the mild devaluation will proportionately reduce the chances of the larger one, and vice versa.

The power of the model to express and handle sophisticated assumptions about devaluation outlooks has now become more apparent.

1. Paul Einzig, *Foreign Exchange Crises:* An Essay in Economic Pathology (New York: 1968), p. 94.
2. David Zenoff: "Environmental Forecasting Is A Tricky Business," *Worldwide P & I Planning* (Sept.–Oct. 1968), pp. 20–27.

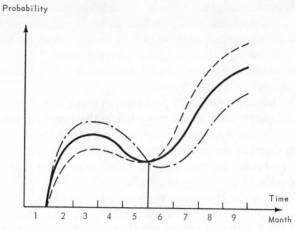

FIGURE 6.3   Effect of Negative Probability Correlations

TABLE 6.2   A "Mild" Negative Correlation Matrix

				k				
m	1	2	3	4	5	6	7	8
1								
2	0.75							
3	0.50	0.75						
4	0.25	0.50	0.75					
5		0.25	0.50	0.75				
6			−0.25	−0.50	−0.75			
7				−0.25	−0.50	0.75		
8					−0.25	0.50	0.75	
9						0.25	0.50	0.75

TABLE 6.3   A "Strong" Negative Correlation Matrix

				k				
m	1	2	3	4	5	6	7	8
1								
2	0.75							
3	0.50	0.75						
4	0.25	0.50	0.75					
5		0.25	0.50	0.75				
6	−1.00	−1.00	−1.00	−1.00				
7	−1.00	−1.00	−1.00	−1.00	−1.00	0.75		
8	−1.00	−1.00	−1.00	−1.00	−1.00	0.50	0.75	
9	−1.00	−1.00	−1.00	−1.00	−1.00	0.25	0.50	0.75

6.2 Correlations of Assets and Liabilities

The theoretical models in Chapters 2 and 3 expressed formally the effect of covariances of assets and liability variables. The most drastic simplification used in the Ace International case was to set all these covariances equal to zero. Business risks of different loan variables, for instance, are often positively correlated. These relationships exist both within time periods and across time periods.

6.2.1 *Correlations Between Liabilities*

The correlation of liabilities within the same time period acknowledges that capital market conditions affect all the sources of credit more or less simultaneously. For example, a bank loan is available 3 months from now at a 15% effective interest cost. The spread of this cost is between 12% and 18%. During the same period, another financial institution makes a line of credit available in the 13% range with a spread between 10% and 16%. If money gets tighter than expected in 3 months, the effective costs of both financing sources will probably be on the higher side of their respective ranges. The random variables expressing the business risks in the 2 cases will be positively correlated.

Also, the correlations stretch across time periods. For instance, one of the banks opens the possibility of a loan in the third and fourth period. If the effective cost in the case of the first loan is underestimated, the same may be true for the second one.

How are correlation coefficients of different financing sources found? Three techniques, increasing in precision, are available. (1) The first one is simply a "guesstimate" of the type just discussed. Logically, credits from similar institutions are highly correlated within the same period, and often even across time periods. Also, loans from the same financial institution are highly correlated over time. (2) The second technique is a regression analysis on a well-established index, like the prime discount rate. The dependent variables are the costs of borrowing at the different institutions over time. The sensitivity of each institution to capital market conditions can be deduced from this analysis. (3) The final, and most precise technique, is a formal covariance analysis of each loan type in each institution. This analysis is efficiently performed by different existing computer programs. All these techniques assume that the past is a good indicator of the future, an assumption that does not necessarily hold. Therefore, these techniques should not be used in a purely mechanical fashion.

6.2.2 *Correlations Between Assets*

Everything that has been said about liabilities can be repeated, *mutatis mutandis*, for assets.

6.2.3 Correlations Between Assets and Liabilities

The correlations between assets and liabilities are often overlooked. In some cases, they are critical ingredients for the model. An important example for short-term financing problems, such as the Ace International case, is the relationship between bond prices and yields. A very strong correlation exists between the market price of bonds and the going interest rate in the capital market.[3]

When the money market gets tighter, the (negative) return of the bank loan will decrease. Similarly, the market value of the treasury bond will move downward. (See Figure 6.4.) This high positive correla-

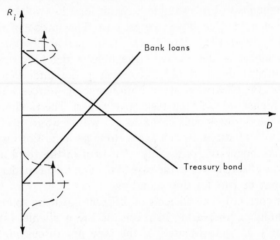

FIGURE 6.4   Correlation Effect Between Bank Loans and Treasury Bonds

tion makes bond transactions a less attractive device to transmit funds from one period to another.

In each case, relationships between the business risks of all variables included in the model should be considered. For practical purposes, however, only the most powerful correlations are integrated in the model.

6.3 Taxation

Taxation in general and international taxation in particular are always complicating factors for decision making, since they can profoundly modify the conclusions. In the Ace International case, only pretax

3. Gerome B. Cohen and Edward Zinbarg, *Investment Analysis and Portfolio Management* (Homewood, Ill.: Richard D. Irwin, 1967), p. 396 (analysis of price and yield of U.S. Government 3% Bonds, due 1995).

expected returns are maximized. Now the model can be expanded to include the tax dimension. Tax structures of increasing complexity can be introduced. The implicit assumption is made that enough income is generated, by operations outside the model if necessary, to show a positive net taxable income. The tax system may be local taxes, U.S. taxes, or a combination of both.

6.3.1 Single Flat Tax Rate on All Returns

For the treatment of the tax dimension, the notation of the model will be modified, because the more general matrix notation is easier to handle than the algebraic one. The model now can be described (subject to all constraints) as

$$\text{maximize } Z = L\mathbf{P}\mathbf{X} - \mathbf{X}^1\mathbf{Q}\mathbf{X}$$

where

L = a scalar, the parameter L of the theoretical models (Chapters 2 and 3).

$\mathbf{P}$ = is an n-component row vector representing the coefficients of the variables in the linear part of the objective function.

$\mathbf{X}$ = an n-component column vector representing all the variables of the model. (The X_{ik} of the theoretical model in Chapter 3.)

$\mathbf{X}^1$ = is the transpose of $\mathbf{X}$.

$\mathbf{Q}$ = is a symmetric n by n matrix containing the coefficients of the quadratic part of the objective function.

If a flat single tax rate applies to all the transactions' profits and losses, the adaptation of the model is straightforward: Let t be the flat single tax rate and let $T = 1 - t$. The model adapted for this tax structure is (subject to all constraints)

$$\text{maximize } Z = TL\mathbf{P}\mathbf{X} - T^2\mathbf{X}^1\mathbf{Q}\mathbf{X}$$

6.3.2 Differential Flat Tax Rates

As a first case of differential taxation, suppose that devaluation losses are not tax deductible. Since financing and hedging decision expenses are tax deductible, the optimal solutions could change drastically. Typically, additional coverage will be purchased to reduce the expected devaluation losses. How will this be integrated into the model? Let $\mathbf{T}$ be an n-by-n diagonal matrix, with only 2 types of entries: 1 and T. The diagonal entries corresponding to the exposure variables are the 1 values; the other diagonal entries contain the T values. All elements of the matrix which are not in the main diagonal are zero. The model adapted for this case (subject to all constraints) is

$$\text{maximize } Z = L\mathbf{PTX} - \mathbf{T}^1\mathbf{X}^1\mathbf{QXT}$$

This same notation, with another $\mathbf{T}$ matrix, represents the generalized differential tax rate problem. Theoretically, every single transaction could be taxed at a different rate. Allowance for different taxations over time are included in this fashion. A new surtax, for instance, would be handled in the model by applying the new rate to all variables relating to the periods in which the surtax exists.

The generalized differential tax rate problem is a flexible tool that will handle a large number of real-life tax systems. There is one major limitation in this technique: It does not allow for tax rates conditional on total profits.

6.3.3 Tax Rates Conditional on Total Profits

The existence of different tax brackets, depending on the total profit figures of the company can make the issues more complex. Assume 3 tax brackets, as in Figure 6.5. The first \$100,000 of net taxable income are taxed at a t_1 rate. A t_2 tax rate applies to the next \$100,000. Finally, any income exceeding this latter boundary is taxed at a flat t_3 rate.

To handle this type of tax structure, a few new variables and constraints are necessary:

$$\text{TAX } 1 = \text{the amount taxable at the } t_1 \text{ rate;}$$
$$\text{TAX } 2 = \text{the amount taxable at the } t_2 \text{ rate;}$$
$$\text{TAX } 3 = \text{the amount taxable at the } t_3 \text{ rate;}$$

and also

$$T_k = 1 - t_k, \qquad k = 1, 2, 3$$

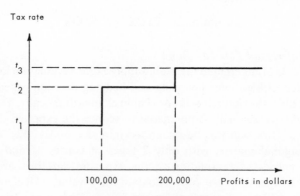

FIGURE 6.5   Tax Bracket System

In the model, these variables are used as follows: The objective function is

$$\text{maximize } Z = \cdots \text{ other terms } \cdots + \sum_{k=1}^{3} T_k \text{TAX } k$$

(see footnote 4) subject to

(other taxable income) $+ \text{PROF} - \text{COST} = \text{TAX } 1 + \text{TAX } 2 + \text{TAX } 3$

where $\text{TAX } 1 \leq 100,000$ and $\text{TAX } 2 \leq 100,000$; and also subject to other constraints.

The variables PROF and COST are the total profits and costs of all the decisions included in the model, as in the Ace International case.

The model, maximizing after-tax expected return, will first apply the lowest tax rate (the highest T_k) to all income up to the maximum allowed to TAX 1. The overflow will be evaluated with the T_2 coefficient up to the maximum of TAX 2. Any balances of taxable income will be weighed by the coefficient T_3. In this fashion, the evaluations of additional profits or cost reductions will automatically take into consideration the tax brackets applying to them.

A combination of the tax bracket technique and differential flat tax rates allows the handling of fairly sophisticated tax structures. Tax exemptions, nondeductible costs, and differential taxes from the previous paragraph can be combined with the tax bracket system explained here.

With no additional effort, the budgeting of the tax payments, deposits, and so forth, could be handled by including the TAX k variables in the cash equations of the relevant periods.

6.4 Changing Profit and Cost Preferences Over Time
With a few minor changes, the model can take into account changing profit and cost preferences over time. For example, applying a subjective discount factor to profits and costs, the model will accordingly shift profits to as early in the planning period as possible and push costs toward the time horizon and beyond.

When this technique is applied on an unwarranted scale, the strategies will be, of course, suboptimal in absolute terms. But myopia is sometimes a voluntary and conscious decision, for "window dressing" or other reasons.

This technique is a necessity when large time units — for example,

---

4. The $\sum_{k=1}^{3} T_k \text{ TAX } k$ represents the after-tax return of the operations.

quarters or years — or long time horizons are involved. A discounted cash flow optimization is then the purpose of the model.

If i is the subjective, or real, discount factor, the only modification required in the model is a redefinition of the variables PROF and COST of Chapter 4. Let

DIPR be the total profit discounted at rate i
DICT be the total costs discounted at rate i

then the model is

maximize $Z = L(\text{DIPR} - \text{DICT}) + \cdots \text{(other terms)} \cdots$

subject to

$$\text{DIPR} = \sum_{k=1}^{T} (1 + i)^{1-k}\text{PRT } k$$

$$\text{DICT} = \sum_{k=1}^{T} (1 + i)^{1-k}\text{CST } k$$

and also subject to other constraints. Here T is the number of time periods of the model (including the "beyond the time horizon" period).

A more extreme case of changing time preferences is the complete neglect of whatever happens beyond the time horizon. This is accomplished simply by dropping the PRT* and CST* variables in the objective function. The model will then purely optimize all cash flows within the time horizon. A typical result will be the accumulation of cost payments beyond the time horizon.

6.5 Mutually Exclusive Decisions

Suppose that the treasurer knows that the bank will open for him a line of credit or a medium-term loan but not both. Or perhaps the central bank will let him choose between a financial swap and an official forward-exchange contract. Similar decision problems arise when the company considers the purchase of mutually exclusive assets, such as licenses from two competitors.

All mutually exclusive decisions can be included in the model. The first technique is, of course, to try the problem once with each variable. The highest return solution, at the same risk level, gives the correct solution. There is a more efficient way to handle these problems than several complete computer runs. The "big M" artifice used for the forward-exchange contracts in the Ace International problem is applicable. If X_1 and X_2 are mutually exclusive decisions, one simply includes M in the objective function $- MX_1X_2$, where M is a very large negative number. Either X_1 or X_2 can be included in the optimal solution but not both, because including both would decrease the objective function one wants to maximize by a large amount.

This option allows one to test, in a single run, the optimal choices between a large number of mutually exclusive variables.

6.6 Contingent Decisions

Government regulations sometimes require contingent decisions. A variable is contingent on other(s) "when acceptance of one proposal is dependent on acceptance of one or more proposals".[5] As examples: Profits can be repatriated for amounts equal to the average holdings of new treasury bonds issued by the government over the last 3 periods; financial swaps are available only for an amount equivalent to 50% of the present outstanding hard-currency loans imported in the country.

To introduce these contingent decisions in the model, only a few new constraints have to be added, using the notation of the Ace International case.

The problem of profit repatriation as subject to treasury bond holdings would be handled for the variable REP 8, for instance, as follows:

$$\text{REP } 8 \leq \frac{(\text{PTB } 6 - \text{STB } 6) + (\text{PTB } 7 - \text{STB } 7) + (\text{PTB } 8 - \text{STB } 8)}{3}$$

The variable REP 8 is constrained to remain less than or equal to the average holdings of treasury bonds over 3 months. This variable will appear in the solution if and only if these holdings are not zero.

The example of financial swaps as contingent on hard-currency imports could be expressed, in the particular case of the financial swap variable FSW 2 (see Section 4.8), as follows:

$$\text{FSW } 2 \leq \text{S\$L } 1 + \text{S\$L } 2 + (\text{old dollar debt outstanding})$$

All other types of contingent decisions can similarly be expressed by inequalities.

The refinements discussed in this chapter have increased the flexibility of the model of the Ace International case. Chapter 7 will delve deeper into some extensions that will complete the model further to the point where it can be operationally used.

5. Martin H. Weingartner: *Mathematical Programming and the Analysis of Capital Budgeting Problems*, (Englewood Cliffs, N. J.: Prentice-Hall, 1963), p. 11. The technique used by Weingartner to deal with contingent problems (p. 33) has been adopted for this model.

7
Extensions of the Ace International Model

Three major extensions of the Ace International model will now be discussed: (1) the use of unequal time periods; (2) the inclusion of capital budgeting; and (3) analysis by simulation of the solution vector. These extensions aim at making the model more flexible for operational use. This chapter concludes with a summary of the model's remaining limitations.

7.1. Unequal Time Periods Model[1]

The general multitemporal model would not be very easy to use on an operational basis, because it requires large amounts of detailed information over extended periods of time. For instance, the treasurer cannot pinpoint his cash requirements for the 15th month as easily as those for next month; and his estimates of maximum amounts of local borrowings at a given rate at more than a year from now are certainly sketchy. Furthermore, he really does not need such detailed information in later periods, because he implements only the first period's output.

At the other extreme, in times of crisis, monthly variables may be too crude for the decisions he has to make. Conditions sometimes change daily, and the Ace International model does not give a time breakdown fine enough to cope with such problems.

An unequal time period model solves these problems. It allows for daily decision variables with very detailed information whenever this information is available or necessary. It also allows the future to be accounted for without too many details, details which are not known.

For example, with only 16 time periods, it is possible to have a

1. The concept of this model was inspired by: Yair Orgler, *An Unequal-Period Model for Cash Management by Business Firms.* Paper presented at the TIMS/ORSA joint meeting, San Francisco, California, May 1968.

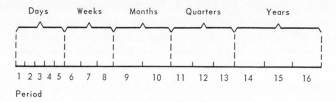

FIGURE 7.1   Unequal Time Periods

4 year total time horizon and still decide on day-to-day matters for the next week. In Figure 7.1, periods 1 through 5 refer to the first 5 working days. The next 3 periods are weeks, then follow 2 monthly periods, 3 quarters, and 3 year periods.

The very detailed information available for next week's decisions can be used in the unequal time period model. The precise timing, on a daily basis, of each operation is given in the output. As these decisions are the only ones that will be implemented, these detailed solutions are welcome. Good insights are also given as to what should be prepared for in the next 3 weeks, and — in the longer run — in the next months and quarters.

The unequal time periods model can be geared exactly to the available and required information. This is its major advantage. If management has some insights on the longer run evolution of the country or the company, this information will fully account for the present decisions. At the same time, daily cash budgets or devaluation information can be fully exploited and can help management make the daily decisions that it has to implement on the spot. Maximum use of all information is guaranteed.

The modifications required to pass from the multitemporal model to the unequal time period model are easily made.

7.2   Capital Budgeting

By the use of the unequal time period model, the capital budgeting problem can finally be tackled. Capital budgeting decisions are usually made on very long time horizons: 5 years, 10 years, and sometimes more. In the multitemporal model with monthly time periods, it would be difficult to evaluate the purchase of a factory with a cash flow that is discounted over 10 years. The unequal time period model solves that difficulty.

The purchase of a factory can be characterized by an expected profit and a variance, in the same manner as treasury bonds. Mutually exclusive or contingent projects are handled in a fashion similar to the techniques described in Sections 6.5 and 6.6. When the projects are correlated to one another, positively or negatively, their covariances will be taken into account. All the refinements of capital budgeting developed with linear programming[2] are directly adaptable to the unequal time period model. In addition, the cash requirement to finance any projects that are accepted can be budgeted, and the adequate financing sources can be determined. The tax dimension can be handled as explained earlier in Section 6.3.

The effects of devaluations on each project have to be determined. The model will evaluate a project with very large working capital requirements in local currency different from another in which hard currency is the major vehicle.

The major advantage of including capital budgeting in the model is that the effects of a project on the cash requirements and on the net exposure are taken into account formally. Two projects with an identical internal rate of return, but with a different timing in the cash flows or the net exposure effect, may be evaluated differently. If one of these projects yields a cash inflow in a period where cash is scarce, or reduces the exposure when a devaluation is imminent, it will be preferred over the others.

The first step in including capital budgeting in the model is the computation of the internal rate of return of each project and the variance of this internal rate of return. The internal rate of return for an investment proposal is the discount rate that equates the present value of the expected cash outflows with the present value of the expected inflows. Computer programs exist that give the internal rate of return from a cash flow forecast. When these programs are not available, tables can be used.[3] The variance is deduced from the computation of the lowest and the highest possible internal rates of return. More sophisticated methods exist to estimate the variance of a proposal. Hillier[4] and Hertz[5] developed techniques to improve these estimates.

An example will illustrate the next steps required in order to include capital budgeting in the model. Two proposals are considered: Project 1 has an internal rate of return r_1 and a variance V_1. Similarly, the

2. See Martin Weingartner, *Mathematical Programming and the Analysis of Capital Budgeting Problems* (Englewood Cliffs, N. J.: Prentice-Hall, 1963).
3. J. Van Horne, *Financial Management and Policy* (Englewood Cliffs, N. J.: Prentice-Hall, 1968), pp. 31–41.
4. Frederick Hillier, "The Derivation of Probabilistic Information for the Evaluation of Risky Investments," *Management Science* vol. 9, no. 3, (April 1963), pp. 443–457.
5. David Hertz, "Risk Analysis in Capital Investment," *Harvard Business Review* vol. 42 (January–February 1964), pp. 95–106.

TABLE 7.1   Cash Flows and Exposures of Two Investment Projects

| | Project 1 | | Project 2 | |
	Cash Flows ($)	Exposure ($)	Cash Flows ($)	Exposure ($)
Period 1	−100,000	—	—	—
Period 2	−20,000	—	−120,000	—
Period 3	+50,000	+50,000	+110,000	+55,000
Period 4	+60,000	+60,000	+50,000	+25,000
Period 5	+40,000	+40,000	+20,000	+10,000
Period 6	+20,000	+20,000	—	—

internal rate r_2 and variance V_2 relate to Project 2. The cash flow and its exposure effects are shown in Table 7.1. These cash flows are supposedly independent of one another.[6] We define X_1 as the percentage of Project 1 accepted. This set of variables is constrained by $0 \le X_i \le 1$, where $i = 1, 2$. These investment projects are included in the model with the notation of the Ace International case. The objective function is

Maximize $Z = r_1 X_1 + r_2 X_2 - V_1 X_1^2 - V_2 X_2^2 + \cdots$ (other terms) $\cdots$

subject to:

CSH 1 = $\cdots$ (other terms) $\cdots - 100,000\ X_1$
CSH 2 = $\cdots$ (other terms) $\cdots - \quad 20,000\ X_1 - 120,000\ X_2$
CSH 3 = $\cdots$ (other terms) $\cdots + \quad 50,000\ X_1 + 110,000\ X_2$
CSH 4 = $\cdots$ (other terms) $\cdots + \quad 60,000\ X_1 + 40,000\ X_2$

and so on. Also,

EXP 3 = $\cdots$ (other terms) $\cdots + 50,000\ X_1 + 55,000\ X_2$
EXP 4 = $\cdots$ (other terms) $\cdots + 60,000\ X_1 + 25,000\ X_2$

and so on, where $0 \le X_1 \le 1$, and $0 \le X_2 \le 1$. There are two major sources of inaccuracy in this approach: the assumption about the reinvestment of the generated funds and the assumption of the indivisibility of investment proposals.

The use of the internal rate of return as an evaluator of the desirability of a project assumes that the funds generated by this project are to be reinvested in projects with yields identical to the internal

6. If cash flows or, more generally, full projects are correlated, this could be taken into account by assigning one variable to each cash inflow or outflow in each period and correlating them.

rate of return. This assumption is only rarely valid. The solution to this problem uses the Hertz simulation approach to compute the expected yield and variance of a given project.[7] The mean yield is then used in the model instead of the internal rate of return.

The second limitation is the problem of divisibility of investment projects. The model could judge, as an optimal solution, to take 25% of project 1 and 60% of project 2. In some cases, when projects can be subdivided, this is a reasonable answer. But when project 1 is a toll bridge over a river, it does not take much sense to build a quarter of a bridge. The problem of divisibility is common to all noninteger programs. Weingartner[8] has made a detailed study of this question. When an integer quadratic programming algorithm is developed, the indivisibility of investment proposals will be solved. Until then, approximations will be required.

7.3 Simulation of the Solution Vector

7.3.1 *Why Simulation?*
Two main reasons justify the analysis by simulation of the solution vector: First, the present output does not indicate *when* the variances on costs or returns occur if one follows a given strategy. Second, the shape of the distribution of the costs or returns of a financing and hedging strategy is useful information to the decision maker and is not available by any other means than simulations.

The information on the timing of the variances can be critical. Consider an extreme example in order to stress this point. The total variance of a 9 month strategy corresponds to a possible loss of $1,000,000 with a given probability. If all of this variance is generated in the ninth month's decisions, the risk is not as large as it appears. The treasurer implements only the first month's decisions. The revised problem is solved again the next month, and so on. By the time the ninth month's decisions are to be implemented, a large part of the uncertainty may have resolved itself. At the other extreme of timing, the $1,000,000 possible loss is attached to the first month. The risk incurred in implementing the suggested solution is now very serious indeed. The knowledge of when the major variances appear can, therefore, add important insights to the solution.

The second reason for using a simulation is to determine the exact shape of the cost or profit distributions of the strategies. In the inter-

7. Hertz, "Risk Analysis," pp. 95–106.
8. Weingartner, *Mathematical Programming*, Chapters 4 and 5.

pretation of the results of all the problems, it has been assumed that the total strategy probability distribution approximated a normal distribution (see Section 1.4.1). This assumption will not often be realistic. The probability distribution of the returns in each period can be deduced from the unitemporal model.

For example, in a given period with a devaluation probability P and a sizable net exposure, the distribution of the return of the strategy might be shaped as in Figure 7.2. If a devaluation does not occur,

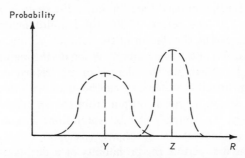

FIGURE 7.2   Probability Distribution of Strategy Return in One Period

the return is somewhere in the distribution around Z. Only business risks generate a deviation from the expected value Z. If a devaluation occurs, the return is distributed around Y. In that case, both the business risk and the uncertainty about the devaluation amount create deviation from the expected value Y. The spread of this distribution is, therefore, larger than the previous one. The area under the distribution around Y corresponds to the devaluation probability P. The other distribution represents a probability $1 - P$. The relative size of each distribution is determined by this devaluation probability, the devaluation amount, and the net exposure. Their spread is a function of the business risk variance and the devaluation variance.

When the "strategy variance" was referred to in earlier chapters, both distributions were taken into account simultaneously. It was assumed previously that the combination of these 2 distributions is approximately a normal distribution. When does this assumption hold?

Obviously, when the probability of a devaluation is 100%, the distribution around Z disappears. Conversely, when the devaluation probability is zero, the distribution around Y vanishes. The same effect exists when the net exposure is zero: The impact of a devaluation on the return is nil in these circumstances. Approximating the total return distribution by a normal curve will be valid in the extreme circumstances listed: a negligible devaluation probability, or devaluation

amount, and/or negligible net exposure. Whenever these parameters
are not zero, the normal distribution is not a valid approximation for
the shape of the probability distribution of strategy returns. A more
general approach is required; the Monte Carlo simulation is the suggested
approach.

7.3.2   *Monte Carlo Simulation of the Solution Vector*

The aim of the Monte Carlo simulation is to yield a set of probability
distributions for the returns. Each month's distribution will be plotted
as in Figure 7.2. The return of the total multitemporal strategy is
similarly plotted. The simulation of the solution vector answers, therefore, two questions at the same time: "When do the major uncertainties
appear?" and, "What are the shapes of the return distributions?"
Very precise probability statements can be made with this information.

Figure 7.3 shows a typical output from the simulation of a three-
period strategy. To simplify the interpretation, assume that in this
problem the amount of the devaluation remains constant over the 3
periods. In the first period, the probability of a devaluation is zero, or
the net exposure is zero, or both are zero. The uncertainty about the
return is caused only by business risks. The lowest possible return is
A_1. In the second period, the net exposure and the devaluation probability are no longer negligible. The resulting distribution becomes more
complex. A return as low as A_2 becomes possible. In the third period,
the deformation is very strong, because of the possibility of high
devaluation losses. A negative return results at A_3, for example.

The total strategy return distribution is a combination of the 3
previous distributions.[9] With graphs of this nature, the interpretation
of a given optimal strategy becomes much more precise.

How does Monte Carlo simulation help us in obtaining these plots?
A Monte Carlo simulation approximates the solution to the problem
by sampling from a random process. By computing a few hundred or
a few thousand times the return of a given optimal solution for the
different possible values of the devaluation amount, the different costs
and profits for the decision variables, and so forth, a distribution of the
return is generated. Another subroutine transforms these data into a
plot diagram printed directly by the computer.

It is helpful to go over this description in more detail. The Monte
Carlo method makes it possible to choose a simulated value for each of
the random variables and to compute the total cost or profit for a given

---

9. It would be the arithmetic mean of the 3 unitemporal distributions if all correlations over time were neglected.

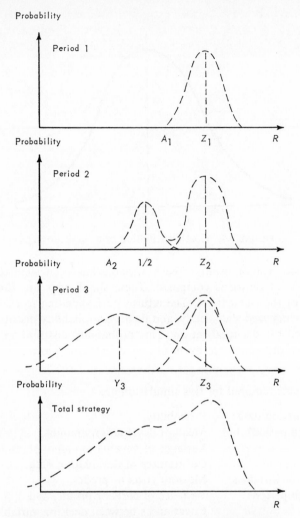

FIGURE 7.3   Simulation of a Three-Period Strategy

strategy. For a bank loan with a mean cost of 20% and the extreme points of a normal distribution at 15% and 25%, the simulated value could be any percentage between 15 and 25 (Figure 7.4). For example, at the first simulation, this value is 18%. The second simulation could be 23%, and then 20% or 15%, and so on. The Monte Carlo method will choose these values in a random fashion, with a guarantee that, after a very large number of simulations, the probability of each percentage approximates the distribution of Figure 7.4.

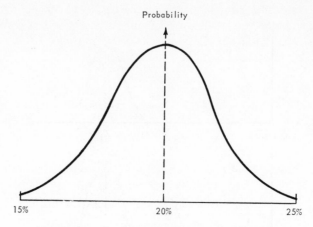

FIGURE 7.4   Cost Distribution of a Bank Loan

Once the cost or profit of each variable has been simulated, the resulting total return is computed. These simulations are run a few hundred or thousand times. The returns corresponding to each simulation are analyzed statistically, and finally a probability distribution is determined for the total return. This probability distribution is then plotted by the computer by means of one of the plotting packages available.

The inputs required for this simulation are

1. Devaluation data: Probability,
   (each period)   Mean of devaluation amount,
                          Variance of devaluation amount, and
                          Covariances of devaluation data.
2. Decision variables: Mean of costs or profits,
   (each period)   Variance of costs or profits, and
                          Covariances between decision variables.
3. Net exposure for each period in the selected strategy.
4. Amounts of each decision variable in the selected strategy.

The first 2 sets of inputs are identical to the input requirements for the devaluation-hedging model itself (see Section 1.3). The last two data requirements are found in the output of the devaluation-hedging model. All these data are entered into the simulation model, which will yield a list of all the simulated returns of each period R_k, and the resulting total strategy return R. The plots of the probability distributions of all the R_k and R are also produced.

The Monte Carlo simulation technique itself will not be explained here. Several good manuals are available,[10] and standard computer packages exist. Only the use of this method to simulate the solution vector is discussed here.

7.3.3 *The Unitemporal Case*

The simulation starts with a random selection of a devaluation amount from the distribution shown in Figure 7.5. (A flow diagram of the simulation of a unitemporal optimal strategy is displayed later in Figure 7.6.)

With this devaluation amount and the net exposure given by the selected optimal strategy, the devaluation losses are computed.[11] The simulation continues by selecting, at random, cost or profit coefficients for all the decision variables of the problem. The total return of the strategy before devaluation is then computed, using the simulated cost and profit coefficients and the amounts of the decision variables given by the selected optimal strategy. Finally, the net return after devaluation losses R is computed and printed.

The computer will go over this process a few hundred or thousand times (S times in Figure 7.6), each time with a new simulated devaluation amount and new profit and cost coefficients. The strategy return R will be computed, accordingly, a few hundred or a few thousand times. The shape of the distribution of these simulated R is what is sought. The distribution of the R is analyzed and plotted by the computer.

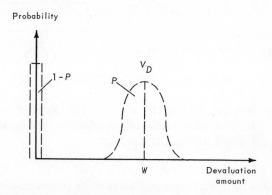

FIGURE 7.5 Probability Distribution of Devaluation Amounts

10. For example: J. M. Hammersley and D. C. Handscomb, *Monte Carlo Methods* (New York: John Wiley and Sons, 1964).

11. When the devaluation amount drawn from the distribution in Figure 7.5 is zero, no devaluation losses occur. The devaluation losses are simply (net exposure) × (devaluation amount).

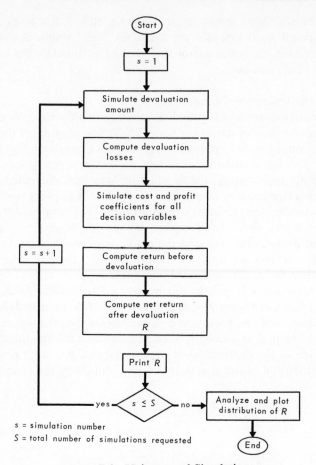

FIGURE 7.6   Unitemporal Simulations

Since the problem of correlations between decision variables to simulate the random cost and profit coefficients has been solved in other works,[12] it will not be discussed here.

7.3.4   *The Multitemporal Case*

The extension to a multitemporal simulation is straightforward. The *T* periods are simulated in the same fashion as in the unitemporal case, and the total multitemporal strategy returns are computed after every *T* cycle. The flow diagram of Figure 7.7 explains the process.

12. C. H. Springer et al.: *Probabilistic Models*, Vol. 4 of Mathematics for Management Series, (Homewood, Ill.: Richard D. Irwin, Inc., 1968), pp. 172–180; also pp. 292–294, where the MONCAR computer program is listed.

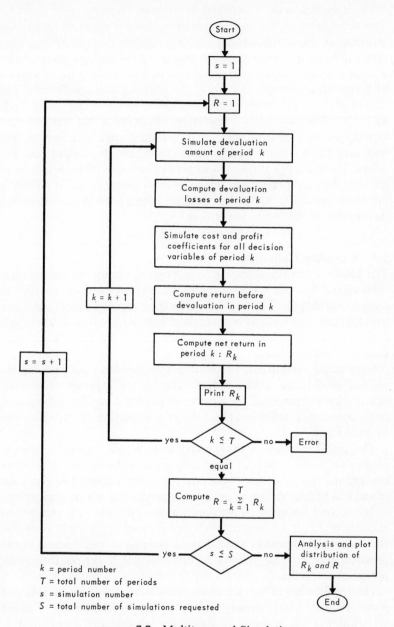

FIGURE 7.7 Multitemporal Simulations

7.3.5   *Conclusions on Simulations of Solution Vectors*
The simulation of the optimal solution vectors produces interesting information about the selected solution. Distributions of returns over time can be an important factor in evaluating the real risk presented by a given strategy. The simulation can also be used to drop the constraint of a two-parameter distribution of the profit or cost coefficients. The shapes of the distributions of the devaluation amounts and of the profit and cost coefficients can be completely custom made. No mathematical expression, or the constraint of a two-parameter distribution, are necessary for a Monte Carlo simulation. Therefore, testing how the return would change if the cost or profit coefficient distributions were different does not present any difficulty. Such testing could be especially important for capital budgeting problems, where uncertainties about the distribution of the return are critical.

7.4   Remaining Limitations
The previous chapter discussed a number of extensions and adaptations of the Ace International model and further ones are covered in the present chapter. The problems that the expanded model can solve with all these new options become more and more involved. There still remain some limitations in the structure of this model, however, and these are now discussed.

Four major limitations, which cannot be avoided even with the expanded model, are acknowledged: the use of expected-value constraints; measurement of the concept of risk by a variance; the use of two-parameter distributions; and the approximation of variable costs by fixed costs.

The first limitation is fairly important. When maximum amount constraints were expressed on loans, cash budgets, and any other constraints, expected values were used for these amounts. The expanded model can handle variances on costs or profits but not on constraints.

The second limitation is a theoretical one: the use of a variance as measure of risk is a heuristic. No better measure is presently available. But it should be borne in mind that the hedging model, because of the heuristic character of the risk measure, is not a perfect theoretical optimization model.

The requirement of two-parameter distributions to express cost and profit estimates has already been discussed (Chapter 1). Further empirical work is required to determine whether this assumption is valid. This limitation is not as critical as the two preceding limitations.

Finally, the fixed costs involved in any operation have to approximate as variable costs. This limitation is common to all noninteger programming techniques.

Of these 4 limitations, the first one is considered to be the most important. In operational use, very often it is desirable to express uncertainties about maximum or minimum constraints. The only solution to this problem with the present technique is to solve the problem several times with different values in the constraints.

The major remaining limitations of the expanded model have been listed. The practical use of this model can now be discussed in Chapter 8.

8
Operational Use of the Model

This chapter will discuss how the theoretical devaluation-hedging model and the case study have to be modified for use in a corporate environment as an ongoing system.

The scope of the model has been reduced to a short-term financing and hedging model. The extensions of the previous chapter are not explicitly used, but this operational model is set up to allow later refinements and additions.

8.1 Theoretical Versus Practical Use

In the theoretical work performed in the previous chapters, emphasis was placed on accuracy and completeness. In practice, these aims are not initially important. The most important objective becomes the objective of the user, that is, the treasurer. The treasurer wants to make decisions and must make them quickly. He does not want to get entangled in abstract concepts such as variances or covariances or in complex operations research considerations. He speaks the financial language and wants reports in this language and not in lists of variables. The efficiency and speed of the computer work also assumes more importance in this setting, especially if computer time is purchased from a computer leasing service. What will all this mean for the use of the devaluation-hedging model?

The first major problem is the concept of risk as handled by the model. The use of a variance is a handy mathematical tool but does not answer the treasurer's question: What is my risk with this specific strategy? Section 8.2 is devoted to the modification of the code to deal with this question. It is shown that this modification also reduces computer time requirements.

The second difficulty is the manipulation of the input and output of the code. A financing and hedging problem involves many variables.

Each transaction has to be analyzed and translated into operations research terms (as was done in Chapter 4). This operations research problem has to be translated, in turn, into input data for the QPS (quadratic programming system) code. After the problem is solved, a translation from the output listings into financial language must be performed (see Chapter 5). Each translation requires time and is often subject to errors. An automatic translation system is needed in which the treasurer presents the data in financial terms and gets the results from the computer in financial language. This topic is discussed in Sections 8.3 and 8.4.

Finally, a description of the model's use as an ongoing system is given in Section 8.5. How all the building blocks fit into one another to run a specific financing and hedging problem and when the problem should be resolved are also discussed.

8.2 The Concept of Risk Revisited

For a treasurer, risk is not a variance. A more satisfactory concept to him is the maximum possible loss with a given probability. If the return or cost distribution of the total strategy were normally distributed, the derivation of the required information would be easy. We have shown in Section 7.3 that this is only rarely true. The theoretical answer to this problem was given earlier: a Monte Carlo simulation of the solution vector. In practice, a shortcut is taken to reduce computer time.

Before going further, it is necessary to stress a consequence of the use of the concept of maximum loss as a measure of risk: The number of optimal strategies that are relevant is reduced. To demonstrate this, we consider an example.

Figure 8.1 shows an efficient frontier with optimal strategies indicated. This presentation is the usual expected-return versus variance approach. The same strategies can be represented in another fashion (see Figure 8.2). For each of the optimal strategies, the worst possible and the best possible outcomes are computed. The expected outcome is also represented.

The concept of maximum possible loss can now be applied to measure the risk of each strategy. It turns out that strategies A, B, and C become irrelevant in light of this new criterion. Strategy A, for example, has an expected cost of $2,000, with a very low variance. The worst possible event would bring these costs to $2,200. Strategy B has an expected cost of only $1,000 but a higher variance. The worst possible outcome would cost $1,600.

One concludes that strategy B is *always* preferable to strategy A,

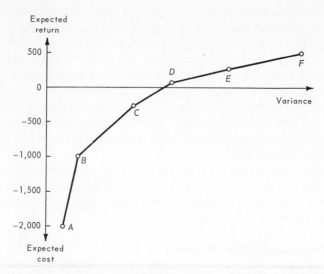

FIGURE 8.1   Efficient Frontier Presentation of Optimal Solutions

which is a fact that the expected-return versus variance representation did not reveal. The same reasoning is relevant for Strategies *B* and *C* in regard to strategy *D*. Strategy *D* will always be preferable to *A*, *B*, or *C*, because its expected cost *and* its maximum loss are both lower.

By using the maximum-possible-loss criterion, from the optimal

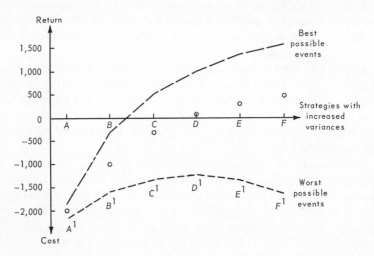

FIGURE 8.2   Presentation of Optimal Strategies with Best and Worst Possible Outcomes

strategies produced by the model, only 3 strategies remain relevant: *D*, *E*, and *F*. This reduces the number of strategies that the model has to generate and, thus, the computation time required.[1]

The QPS code has been internally modified to screen out all strategies that are not relevant. This is done through a search procedure that determines the optimal strategy with the minimum possible loss (i.e., it determines point D^1 in the worst possible event curve of Figure 8.2).

Once this point has been determined, the corresponding *L* parameter is computed. The code generates all strategies from this minimum-possible-loss optimal strategy *D* to the complete expected-return maximization ($L = \infty$).

Typically, in large problems, over 75% of the strategies do not have to be computed. Only the upper end of the efficient frontier remains relevant (in our example, strategies *D*, *E*, and *F*). This reduces computation time significantly.

In summary, the criterion of maximum possible loss as a measure of risk reduces the number of relevant optimal strategies of the efficient frontier. The QPS code is modified to compute only the optimal strategies that remain relevant with the maximum-possible-loss criterion.

It is now necessary to define with more precision what that maximum possible loss of a given strategy means. Intuitively, it is the cost of the strategy if all the worst possible events occur. Technically, it is the cost of a portfolio of decisions, when the random variables of each decision are all in their worst possible configuration.

For a unitemporal strategy, the worst possible event is that all financing and hedging costs should be at the high end of their distributions, and all profit-making transactions at the low end of theirs, and that a devaluation occurs of the maximum amount. The ends of the distributions can be considered, for all practical purposes, as falling at a distance of three standard deviations from the mean.[2]

For a multitemporal strategy, the worst possible event is that, in all periods, the financing and hedging costs are at their worst and the devaluation occurs when the devaluation losses are the highest. These devaluation losses are simply the product of the net exposure of the period and the highest possible devaluation amount.

For instance, in a multitemporal strategy of 4 months, the maximum possible loss for each month and the full 4 months' strategy are given

1. This reduction of optimal strategies is also relevant in portfolio theory.
2. There is less than 0.5% probability that the random variables are beyond 3 standard deviations in a normal distribution.

TABLE 8.1   Maximum Costs of a Four-Month Strategy

Month	Maximum Financing and Hedging Cost	Minimum Profit- Making Transactions	Maximum Devaluation Loss	Maximum Total Loss
1	$2,000	($500)	$1,000	$2,500
2	$3,000	($200)	$2,000	$4,800
3	$2,000	($100)	$1,500	$3,400
4	$1,000	(0)	$1,000	$2,000
Total Strategy	$8,000	($800)	$2,000	$9,200

in Table 8.1. The maximum total losses of the full 4 months' strategy are smaller than the sum of the maximum total losses of each month's strategy. The reason for this is simply that a devaluation could only happen once in the next 4 months. The maximum devaluation loss in each month is part of the maximum total losses of that month. The maximum possible devaluation loss in the 4 month strategy is only $2,000, or the highest amount in the 4 months.

In the code, the multitemporal maximum possible loss is the one that is relevant. But in the output, both unitemporal and multitemporal maximum losses are given.

8.3   The Input Generator

The objective of the input generator is to translate financial data automatically into input for the quadratic programming system code. The use of an input generator allows the executive who is not familiar with the QPS code to solve a problem from data expressed in such financial terms as interest costs, maturities, installments, and so forth.

The input generator is a complete program that prepares all the cards required to run the QPS code. The input of this program is a set of cards giving the relevant financial parameters for each transaction. Its output is a card deck or a tape that will be used as input to the QPS code itself. In addition, some information computed in the input generator is stored on disc for later use by the output generator.

Figure 8.3 explains how the programs relate to one another. The input deck of the input generator is the set of cards, one for each transaction, with the input data in financial language. Typically, this deck contains a few hundred cards and is processed by the input generator program. Two types of output are delivered by this program. The first is the full set of cards required for the quadratic programming system (QPS),

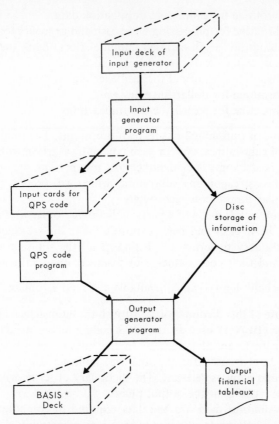

FIGURE 8.3   Relationship Between Input Generator, QPS Code, and Output Generator

representing from 2,000 to 10,000 cards, depending on the size of the problem. Obviously, using a tape instead of cards is a logical alternative for this output. The second output from the input generator program is stored on disc. This information will be retrieved when the problem has been solved completely. The output generator program requires additional data for printing the financial tableaux and will call the disc at that time to obtain this information. The outputs of the output generator program are discussed in Section 8.4.

What is the input generator program? It is a program with a set of subroutines that are individually enlisted, or "called," by identification numbers on the input cards. Examples of such subroutines are:

A subroutine for punching all the cards that are always required by the QPS code: control cards, exposure constraints, and so forth.

A subroutine for processing devaluation data.

A subroutine for processing basic cash and exposure forecast data.

A subroutine for all exposed liabilities (local bank loans, private loans, export-draft discounting, and so on).

A subroutine for normal forward exchange contracts.

A subroutine for dollar financing.

A subroutine for treasury bond transactions.

Each type of transaction has its own subroutine. The total represents a library of subroutines, one for each type of transaction with which the company is dealing. The identification number on the input cards will call the corresponding subroutine, which will process the data of the particular transaction accordingly.

The input deck is made of 4 parts: a dictionary of terms, the devaluation data, basic cash and basic exposure data, and transactions data.

The dictionary of terms is a listing of all the transaction decision variables and their code names. For instance, one dictionary item is:

BLA 1 = bank loan, type A, available at Credit Lyonnais, month 1.

The purpose of this dictionary is to furnish the equivalence between the code name (BLA 1) used in the QPS code and the meaning of this transaction in financial language. In the output generator, only the financial idiom is used for the financial tableaux. In the QPS code, only the code name is relevant. The dictionary of terms will be stored on disc for retrieval at the output phase.

The devaluation data are the data required to compute all of the coefficients involving devaluation probability and amounts. Each period has a card, on which the following data are entered:

Devaluation probability,

Most likely devaluation amount,

Maximum possible devaluation amount, and

Minimum possible devaluation amount.

In addition, the devaluation data correlation matrix is entered. These cards will call the subroutine that computes the mean devaluation amount, the variances, and the covariances. The corresponding cards are punched for the QPS code, and some of these data are stored on disc. These latter data will be used to compute devaluation losses and maximum devaluation losses in the output generator program.

The third data set is simply one card giving each month's basic cash requirement and basic exposure. The subroutine for processing such information is called. These data are used only in the QPS code.

The last data set is the most important one: that for all financing and hedging transactions. Each type of transaction is identified with a code number to call the relevant subroutine. Each transaction is represented by one card. Typical data entered on these cards:

Code name,

Identification number,

Most likely cost (or return),

Minimum possible cost (or return),

Maximum possible cost (or return),

Period in which transaction is available,

Period in which transaction matures,

Maximum amount,

Correlations with other transactions, and

Optional other constraints: for example, mutual exclusiveness with other transactions, contingency, and so forth.

These transaction data cards call the corresponding subroutines to compute means, variances, and covariances, and to create the relevant constraints.

All these data are expressed directly in terms of financial parameters or easily understandable concepts that an executive without operations research specialization can handle. From his point of view, this is the only contact he has with the computer. All the rest will be performed automatically.

The first operation accomplished by the input generator program is a number of checks for internal consistency. Have all the critical data been entered? Are there conflicting transactions?

It is only after the data have been checked for internal consistency that the input generator program commences the operations of processing the data, punching the cards, and loading the disc with the appropriate data.

New subroutines will have to be added to the input generator program when new types of transactions arise. With 20 to 50 types of transactions, most of the existing financial and hedging possibilities can be covered. The total number of subroutines in the library of the input generator program will therefore remain manageable.

8.4 The Output Generator

The output generator is automatically called when optimal solutions are reached by the QPS code. The input of the output generator is the optimal solution vector and the information stored on disc (see Figure 8.3).

Two different outputs are generated by this program. The first one

TABLE 8.2 Financing and Hedging Strategy in France (May 1969–May 1970)
(transactions in thousands of dollars)

	Month 1	Month 2	Month 3
LOCAL FINANCING			
(Old Debt Outstanding)	15,500	10,000	6,000
Bank Loan			
Type *A*, available at Credit Lyonnais	3,000	3,000	5,000
Type *B*, available at Banque de Paris		5,000	2,000
Export Draft Discounting	2,000	1,500	1,000
Private Loan Company *Y*		1,000	
	. . . .	. . .	. . .
TOTAL LOCAL FINANCING	22,000	23,000	22,000
FOREIGN FINANCING			
Dollar Financing	3,000	4,000	2,000
Deutschemark Financing	500	250	200
TOTAL FOREIGN FINANCING	3,500	4,250	2,200
TOTAL FINANCING	25,500	27,250	24,200

TABLE 8.2—(*Continued*)

	Month 1	Month 2	Month 3
PURE HEDGING TRANSACTIONS			
Forward Exchange Contracts	11,000	10,000	10,000
Excess Inventory Hedging	300	200	200
TOTAL PURE HEDGING	11,300	10,200	10,200
OTHER TRANSACTIONS			
Treasury Bonds on Hand	3,000		6,000
Cash on Hand	500	400	400
EXPOSURE EFFECTS			
Basic Exposure	13,300	22,800	19,300
Decrease (increase) by local financing transactions	6,500	13,000	16,000
Decrease (increase) by pure hedging transactions	11,300	10,200	10,200
Increase (decrease) by cash and bonds transactions	3,500	400	6,400
Resulting Exposure	1,000	0	500

is a small card deck, called BASIS*, which contains all information to start the QPS code from that point. If the treasurer, after obtaining a specific optimal solution, wants to make some changes in the assumptions, he does not have to start off the QPS code from the beginning. The BASIS* deck allows him to start at the last optimal solution. New optimal solutions will be obtained with this deck in a matter of seconds.[3]

The second output is the full description of the optimal strategy, with an additional work sheet containing all cost and risk data. This output is on paper and in the format of financial tableaux. There will be one output of this form for each optimal solution generated by the QPS code.

The description of an optimal strategy is a financial tableau with all the transactions given in full, stating which bank loans are outstanding in any given month, which forward-exchange contracts are outstanding, etc. Such subtotals as total local financing, total foreign financing, total financing, and total forward-exchange contracts outstanding are also computed. The treasury bonds outstanding and the cash on hand in each month are represented. Finally, the exposure effects of all the transactions and the net resulting exposure are computed.

An example of such a financial table is given in Table 8.2, showing only the first 3 months of the planning period. For a 12 month strategy, the computer will print out 12 such monthly columns.

A cost and risk working sheet is also printed. It contains all the data necessary for choosing between different optimal strategies. Expected costs are computed separately each month for financing, hedging, and devaluation. Maximum costs at a probability of 5% are given for each strategy as a measure of the risk. Similarly, maximum costs at a 0.5% probability are given to represent the extreme high end of the distribution. Cumulative costs are also computed. These cumulative costs are the costs one incurs for hedging until a devaluation occurs.

All this information is supplied to help the treasurer choose among different optimal strategies. An example of the data in a cost and risk work sheet for a specific strategy is shown in Table 8.3.

The output, as can be seen in the examples, is completely expressed in financial language. The concept of variance is replaced by computations of maximum costs with given probability. The lists of variables describing a strategy are replaced by a financial tableau that is readily understandable by any financial officer.

3. Over 90% of the computation time in the QPS code is used to obtain a first optimal solution.

TABLE 8.3 Cost and Risk Work Sheet Financing and Hedging in France (May 1969–May 1970) (transactions in thousands of dollars)

	Month 1	Month 2	Total Policy
EXPECTED COST			
Financing Expected Costs	1,500	1,000	8,500
Hedging Expected Costs	600	800	4,000
Total Transactions Cost	2,100	1,800	12,500
Expected Devaluation Loss	0	100	600
TOTAL EXPECTED COSTS	2,100	1,900	13,100
MAX. COSTS (Probability 5%)			
Financing Max. Costs	2,600	2,300	12,600
Hedging Max. Costs	900	1,200	7,000
Total Max. Transactions Costs	3,100	3,500	19,600
Max. Devaluation Loss	0	950	950
TOTAL MAX. COSTS	3,100	44,50	20,550
MAX. COSTS (Probability $\frac{1}{2}$%)			
Financing Max. Costs	3,100	2,600	13,400
Hedging Max. Costs	950	1,250	7,900
Total Max. Transactions Costs	4,050	3,850	21,300
Max. Devaluation Loss	0	1,060	1,060
TOTAL MAX. COSTS	4,050	4,910	22,360
CUMULATIVE MAX. COSTS (Probability 5%)			
Total Max. Transactions Costs	3,100	6,600	19,600
Max. Devaluation Loss	0	950	950
TOTAL CUMULATIVE COSTS	3,100	7,550	20,550

8.5   The Use of the Model as an Ongoing System

Now the successive steps required to run a specific problem can be described. First, all the required information has to be gathered. Some of these data come from overseas: for instance, availability of loans, details on government controls. Outside bankers and economists can be consulted about devaluation probabilities and amounts. Cash forecasts and exposure forecasts are prepared.

When all the information has been gathered, it is analyzed and the input generator deck is punched. From the treasurer's point of view, the next step is the interpretation of the output: the financial tableaux and cost-risk working sheets. It is advisable at this point for the treasurer to review the assumptions of the most important transactions recommended in the solution by asking questions such as the following: Are the cost assumptions of this $5 million loan correct? Is the maximum amount on this constraint as strict as assumed? Sensitivity analysis can help screen out constraints and variables that are most critical.

The decision concerning the choice of optimal strategy is made after study of the cost and risk working sheets of each optimal strategy. The transactions of period 1 are then implemented, and the groundwork laid for the future periods.

As soon as major new information is known, the problem has to be solved again with revised data. For example, a change in devaluation probabilities or in government controls, or a reduction in the uncertainty about costs of future transactions, any one of these could make a rerun mandatory.

A fully operational hedging model has now been presented to handle the most frequent foreign exchange crisis: devaluation. However, there is a danger that this technique would be outdated if the present monetary system were modified. The next chapter was prepared to avoid this outdating.

9
Adaptation to Other Foreign Exchange Problems

So far only one type of foreign exchange crisis was considered, namely, devaluations. In fact, as the German mark episode of September 1969 demonstrated, other types of currency adjustments are occurring. The mark first was floated and finally formally revalued. In this chapter, the adaptations of the devaluation-hedging model to all the other types of foreign exchange problems are analyzed and explained.

The first 3 adaptations concern straightforward problems under the present monetary system: revaluations, speculation, and multiple currency hedging. The balance of the chapter is devoted to the potential new monetary systems. As the model is designed to handle only the present monetary system, it could soon be outdated by a new set of rules for the game. The adaptations presented here are designed to prevent this outdating.

Unhappiness about the present monetary system has been voiced in academic circles for many years. Theories supporting the viewpoint of freer markets for foreign exchange have cropped up in a variety of countries. Recently the Bretton Woods agreement, which defined the rules of the present monetary system, has been attacked even in the International Monetary Fund (IMF) itself. The chairman of a meeting at the IMF, Mr. J. M. Dagnino Pastore, complained that "the world monetary system is plagued by recurrent exchange crises, widespread uncertainty, massive and unstabilizing speculation, high and rising interest rates, and even the extension of controls and restrictions."[1]

New rules for the IMF are discussed in virtually every economic or financial journal during the late 1960s. How drastic the reform will be is an unknown at the present writing, but a reform of some kind is very

1. *Wall Street Journal*, September 30, 1969, p. 20.

likely. The most drastic of all the proposed reforms is the complete free market. The floating of the German mark on September 29, 1969 illustrated how this system would function. A less dramatic change is the introduction of the dynamic or crawling pegs (discussed in Section 9.5). At the least-ambitious end of the scale, one finds the proposal of a wider band around the present parity points.

In one of these three changes, or a combination of them, the future of the monetary system seems to lie. The adaptations of the model to all these possibilities can be outlined.

9.1 Revaluations

The frequency of devaluations is much higher than that of revaluations. In the 1948–1967 period, the only currency that showed a net appreciation is the Lebanese pound. But this statistic masks the fact that some currencies devalued and later revalued. The Dutch guilder ,and the German mark fall in this category. The crisis in Europe in late 1968, with the battle between a depreciation of the French franc and an appreciation of the German mark, showed dramatically that the possibility of a currency revaluation should not be overlooked. The actual revaluation of the mark in December 1969 drove this point home once again.

The adaptation of the model to revaluations is straightforward. A revaluation is simply a negative devaluation (Figure 9.1).

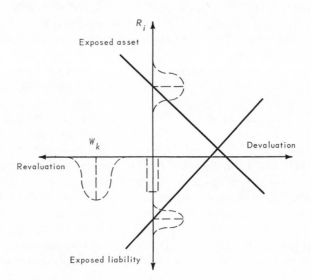

FIGURE 9.1   Effects of a Revaluation on Exposed Assets and Liabilities

An asset whose return is expressed in a currency liable to revalue will increase its return as expressed in dollars after a revaluation. More dollars will be received for the same amount of German marks, if this currency appreciates. The effect on Deutschemark (DM) liabilities under such circumstances would be the same — that is, they are increased. More dollars would be required to repay a DM loan, after a revaluation. In fact, the roles of liabilities and assets are switched when one considers revaluation instead of devaluation.[2]

In terms of the unitemporal or multitemporal model (Chapters 2 and 3), the only step required to adapt the model to revaluations is to change the signs of the W_k coefficients. When $W_k > 0$, the model treats devaluations, and when $W_k < 0$, the model solves revaluation problems.

9.2 Speculation

The model has not been allowed to speculate on a currency depreciation. The constraint that the net exposure should be positive or zero prohibited any form of speculation. This constraint is now dropped.

As a first case, a pure speculation model is considered. In this model, net exposure is never allowed to become positive. Since the computer code assumes automatically that all variables are positive, a new variable is defined. How would the Ace International case be modified into a purely speculative problem? Let SPC k be the net negative exposure of period k, or net speculative exposure of the period. This variable is included in place of EXP k with a change in sign; that is, SPC k = $-$ EXP k. This is the only change required to modify the model into a purely speculative model. Obviously, the solution vector of the Ace International problem would dramatically change.

In the more general case, the model is not constrained at all in the sign of the net exposure. It will speculate when the occasion arises, and allow a positive net exposure when necessary. Since the computer code does not allow variables to become negative, a little artifice is used. Let EXP k minus SPC k (SPC k now being defined as positive) be the net exposure as defined in earlier chapters. The variable EXP k is now simply the sum of all exposed assets. The variable SPC k becomes the sum of all exposed liabilities. Whenever EXP $k >$ SPC k, a positive net exposure results and when EXP $k <$ SPC k, the model is speculating. Both variables EXP k and SPC k remain positive at all times, but their difference — the net exposure — is unconstrained in sign.

2. Notice that a devaluation of the French franc, for instance, is equivalent to a revaluation of all the other currencies for a French company. The revaluation model should therefore be used by international corporations whose home currency devalues.

This last model, without limitations on speculative power, is the more general case. The optimal solutions will often be better in the unconstrained exposure model than in the two previous situations: prohibition of speculation, and compulsory speculation.

Speculation on a currency appreciation is a straightforward combination of the principles presented in Section 9.1 and in this section.

9.3 Multiple Currency Devaluation Hedging

The devaluation of the pound sterling in November 1967 created a typical foreign exchange crisis in which several other currencies followed suit. For example, the Danish krone, the Israeli pound, the Hong Kong dollar, and the New Zealand pound devalued in a chain reaction immediately after the pound sterling. A total of 22 currencies followed suit.

When a company deals in a large number of currencies, these chain reaction devaluations can have serious effects. Solving the devaluation-hedging problem for each currency separately would completely undervalue the real risk. The devaluation probabilities, in the case of chain reaction devaluations, are strongly positively correlated to one another and, therefore, significantly increase the total variance of a strategy.

Another recent foreign exchange crisis, in September 1969, was a case of negative correlations between devaluation and revaluation probabilities. A revaluation of the German mark would have reduced the probability of a devaluation of the French franc, and vice versa. In case of such a major foreign exchange crisis, all the currencies involved should be considered simultaneously.

Hence, the generalization of the model to deal with multiple currency devaluation hedging is presented.[3] The multitemporal case is now stated, as an extension of Chapter 3.

We now define the following variables:

L = parameter varying from 0 to ∞.

E_{ck} = expected return of period k's decisions in currency c.

V_{ck} = variance of period k's decisions in currency c.

R_{ck} = return of period k's decisions in currency c.

C_{ckm} = devaluation covariance between periods k and m in currency c.

D_{ck} = devaluation amount in period k of currency c. ($D_{ck} = W_{ck} + \tilde{C}_{cDk}$).

W_{ck} = expected devaluation amount of period k in currency c.

---

3. Devaluation and revaluation can be considered simultaneously by a combination of Sections 9.1 and 9.3.

X_{cik} = amount of asset or liability i included in portfolio of period k in currency c.

A_{cik} = yield on asset or liability i without taking into account the devaluation of period k in currency c.

$A_{c, N+K}$ = devaluation coefficient of period k in currency c.

$V_{c, N+K}$ = variance of period k of the devaluation coefficient in currency c.

$X_{c, N+K}$ = net exposure in period k in currency c.

P_{ck} = devaluation probability in period k in currency c.

$\tilde{d}_{ck}$ = random variable = 0 if currency c does not devalue in period k;

= 1 if currency c does devalue in period k.

$\tilde{C}_{cDk}$ = random variable with zero mean, measuring uncertainty about the devaluation amount of currency c in period k. The variance is V_{cDk}.

$\tilde{C}_{cik}$ = random variable with zero mean, measuring business risk of variable i in currency c and in period k. The variance is V_{cik}.

N = number of assets and liabilities in period.

T = number of periods.

F = number of currencies.

Assume that a change in devaluation estimates of a specific currency in a given period correlates with the estimates of other currencies only in the same period. For example, a deviation from the expected devaluation probability of the sterling pound in January will create a deviation in the same direction of the Hong Kong dollar in January. For instance, there is no direct effect on the estimates of the Hong Kong dollar in February.[4] Mathematically, this means that for currencies c and f, during periods k and m,

$$\text{cov}\,(\tilde{d}_{ck}\,\tilde{d}_{fm}) = \text{cov}\,(\tilde{C}_{cDk}\,\tilde{C}_{fDm}) = 0$$

where $c \neq f$ and $k \neq m$. Only the covariances of different currencies in the same period are different from zero:

$$\text{cov}\,(\tilde{d}_{ck}\,\tilde{d}_{fk}) \neq 0$$

$$\text{cov}\,(\tilde{C}_{cDk}\,\tilde{C}_{fDk}) \neq 0$$

By calculations similar to the ones in the mathematical appendix,

4. This constraint could be dropped at the price of a more complex correlation matrix.

one proves:

$$\text{cov}\,(R_{ck}R_{fk}) = \sum_{i=1}^{N}\sum_{j=1}^{N} X_{cik}X_{cjk}\,\text{cov}\,(\tilde{C}_{cik}\tilde{C}_{cjk}) + F_{cf}X_{c,N+k}X_{f,N+k}$$

where

$$F_{cf} = W_{ck}W_{fk}\,\text{cov}\,(\tilde{d}_{ck}\tilde{d}_{fk})$$

$$+ \text{cov}\,(\tilde{d}_{ck}\tilde{d}_{fk})\,\text{cov}\,(\tilde{C}_{cDk}\tilde{C}_{fDk}) + P_{ck}P_{fk}\,\text{cov}\,(\tilde{C}_{cDk}\tilde{C}_{fDk})$$

The double summation term,

$$\left[\sum_{i=1}^{N}\sum_{j=1}^{N} X_{cik}X_{cjk}\,\text{cov}\,(\tilde{C}_{cik}\tilde{C}_{cjk})\right],$$

now includes the impact of the correlations of the decision variables across national borders. For example, a rise in the bank rate in Britain can provoke a similar action in Hong Kong or New Zealand. The business risks of local borrowing in those countries are correlated, and the double summation term will take care of this relationship. Capital markets are becoming less impervious to worldwide influences, and correlations of this type will be increasingly important.

The second term, that after the double summation term, $F_{cf}\,X_{c,N+k}$ $X_{f,N+k}$ measures the effects of the correlations of devaluation characteristics of the different currencies. For instance, if it is known that an increase in devaluation probability and amount of the pound sterling creates a proportional reaction in the Hong Kong dollar, then

$$\text{correlation}\,(\tilde{d}_{ck}\tilde{d}_{fk}) = \text{correlation}\,(\tilde{C}_{cDk}\tilde{C}_{fDk}) = 1$$

In the case of a perfect negative correlation between a French devaluation and a German revaluation, these expressions would become -1. These correlations are used to compute the value of F_{cf}.

The general multitemporal, multiple-currency devaluation-hedging model is

$$\text{maximize } Z = L\sum_{c=1}^{F}\sum_{k=1}^{T} E_{ck} - \sum_{c=1}^{F}\sum_{k=1}^{T} V_{ck}$$

$$- \sum_{c=1}^{F}\sum_{k=1}^{T}\sum_{m=1}^{T} C_{ckm}X_{c,N+k}X_{c,N+m}$$

$$- \sum_{c=1}^{F}\sum_{f=1}^{F}\sum_{k=1}^{T}\sum_{m=1}^{T}\sum_{i=1}^{N}\sum_{j=1}^{N} X_{cik}X_{fjm}\,\text{cov}\,(\tilde{C}_{cik}\tilde{C}_{fjm})$$

$$- \sum_{c=1}^{F}\sum_{f=1}^{F} F_{cf}X_{c,N+k}X_{f,N+k} \qquad k \neq m, i \neq j; c \neq f,$$

where

$$E_{ck} = \sum_{i=1}^{N} X_{cik} A_{cik} + X_{c,\,N+k} A_{c,\,N+k} \qquad c = 1, \ldots, F; \; k = 1, \ldots, T$$

$$V_{ck} = \sum_{i=1}^{N} X_{cik}^2 V_{cik} + X_{c,\,N+k}^2 V_{c,\,N+k}$$

$$+ \sum_{i=1}^{N} \sum_{j=1}^{N} X_{cik} X_{cjk} \, \text{cov} \, (\tilde{C}_{cik} \tilde{C}_{cjk}) \qquad i \neq j$$

where

$$c = 1, \ldots, F$$
$$i = 1, \ldots, N$$
$$k = 1, \ldots, T$$

subject to: $X_{cik} \geq 0$, and

$$X_{c,\,N+k} = \sum_{i=1}^{N} X_{cik} B_{cik}, \qquad c = 1, \ldots, F; \; k = 1, \ldots, T$$

and all other constraints.

This model is the most general devaluation-hedging model. The unitemporal and multitemporal models of Chapters 1 and 2 are simply particular cases of the multiple-currency model. At the limit, this general model, with extensions for the speculation option, international taxation, capital budgeting, and unequal time periods, could be used for worldwide allocation of resources based on financial criteria. Which investments should be made, where, and when and in what currency should the funds be raised? Worldwide internal and external financial transactions considered desirable, shifting of funds to tax havens, and so forth, can be handled.

There are no theoretical problems with this general multiple-currency model. Practical use would be impaired by the requirement of a very efficient worldwide management information system which few — if any — companies possess at this time. If and when such an information system exists, improvements of the worldwide financial transactions become possible. For example, funds raised in the European dollar market to finance an investment in Latin America whose profits are transferred by transfer pricing to a tax haven in Panama can be handled and optimized. To consider simultaneously all investment opportunities, long term and short term, and the financing and hedging possibilities is a promising approach. Risk is taken formally into account, and, by simulation of the optimal solution, the uncertainty of each future period is estimated. This approach would be a powerful tool in planning and implementing corporate strategies. This far-reaching technique will probably not be implemented in the near future. The major difficulty is the lack of information systems on a worldwide basis.

In some particular cases, such as the European Common Market, companies have centralized information on their investment opportunities and financial transactions. In times of currency instability, full advantage should be taken of this information by using the multiple-currency model. Even if a worldwide optimization is probably beyond the present practical reach, optimization within geographical areas could become operational very soon.

9.4 Floating Exchanges

The most drastic reform of the present monetary system would be the complete floating of all exchanges. Official intervention points, as specified by the International Monetary Fund at 1 % below and above the official parity of a currency in the spot market, would disappear. Currencies would adjust themselves freely in the market, like any commodity. The experience of the Canadian dollar from 1950 to 1960 and the short episode of the floating of the German mark toward the end of 1969 illustrate how this system would work in practice.

If free markets become a reality for all major world currencies, what implications exist for a treasurer? First of all, hedging will become a systematic problem. Now, only when a foreign-exchange crisis is expected or suspected do normal corporations engage in hedging. Only commodity traders or other businesses operating on very narrow profit margins are perpetual hedgers.

In a world of floating exchange, what is now a behavior of commodity trades will become generalized practice. The use of a more systematic approach to the hedging problem, such as the one advocated in this book for example, would become a critical necessity. How would the model be adapted to a floating exchange monetary system?

In fact, such a system would greatly simplify the mathematical aspect of the model, because the devaluation probability profile is much simpler. Instead of a profile in two parts, as in Figure 2.1 — when one part is discrete (the probability that the devaluation does not occur) and the other continuous (the probability distribution of the amount of devaluation if the devaluation occurs) — only the continuous part would remain.

Discrete devaluations disappear to become continuous fluctuations. The discrete block where nothing happens (as in Figure 2.1 or Figure 9.1) disappears, and the continuous distribution grows to represent

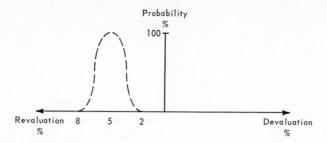

FIGURE 9.2 Probability Profile of the Floating of the German Mark on September 29, 1969

100% of all outcomes. If a currency is expected to float upward, as in the case of the German mark in 1969, or the Canadian dollar in 1970, the currency fluctuation profile would be as represented in Figure 9.2.

The mathematics of the model can be adjusted by fixing the values $\tilde{d} = 1$ and $P = 100\%$ in the theoretical model presented in Chapter 2, and by similarly setting the values d_k and P_k to 1 in Chapter 3. No other changes are required to operate the model under floating exchanges.

9.5 Crawling Peg Proposal

The crawling, or dynamic, peg is an intermediate solution between the fixed rate and the floating exchange. Currencies would be allowed to float within a given margin every month; such floating would permit major adjustments cumulatively over time.

The currency fluctuation profiles to be substituted for the devaluation probability profile would look like Figure 9.3 for 3 successive months. We assume, for instance, that the German mark would have

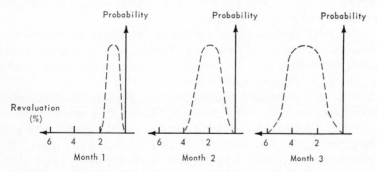

FIGURE 9.3 Probability Profiles of Three Successive Months of Crawling Pegs

gone on a crawling peg within a 2% range per month instead of floating as in Section 9.4. To adapt the model to a crawling peg monetary system, again the values of d_k and P_k would be set at the value 1 in the theoretical model of Chapters 2 and 3. The coefficients W (representing in this case the expected revaluation amount in month 2) would gradually increase over time. The widening spread of the possible revaluation amounts would be captured in the variances of the devaluation coefficient V_{N+k} as in the basic theoretical model. No other changes are required for handling crawling pegs with the devaluation-hedging model.

9.6 Wider Bands Proposal

The weakest proposal to reform the present monetary system consists of increasing the spread between the official intervention points. As stated earlier, presently the maximum deviation from parity allowed by the International Monetary Fund is 1%. This proposal would basically keep the present monetary system but simply allow the deviation from parity to be larger, say 5%. A similar system has been operating for years in Switzerland, for example. The official intervention points of the Swiss franc have been fixed at 2% above and below parity. The implications of a wider band proposal for a treasurer are that even without a formal devaluation nonnegligible fluctuations can occur.

Until now, the loss that could be sustained by a corporation because of movements of the spot rate within the range of the official intervention points has been neglected. The reason for this neglect is that, although theoretically deviations of up to 2% are possible (from one extreme of the range to the other), in reality the vast majority of central banks intervene much earlier than the point at which official intervention is reached. This keeps the actual fluctuations of a currency, when no formal change in parity is made, small enough to be negligible for a large number of corporations.

If the wider band proposal is accepted throughout the world, with intervention points at 5% either way of parity, such fluctuations would become too important to be neglected. A currency fluctuation profile could look like Figure 9.4, for example.

Instead of a discrete probability block centered on the devaluation amount zero as in the basic model of Chapter 2, a new continuous probability distribution appears. In the example of Figure 9.4, there is a 60% probability that a formal devaluation would not occur. The fluctuations of the currency would then be limited to the range -5% to $+5\%$.

A second continuous probability distribution, this one identical to

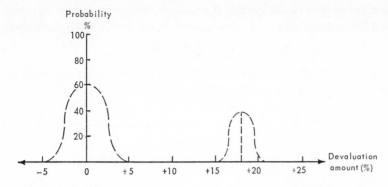

FIGURE 9.4   Currency Fluctuation Profile under the Wider Band Proposal

the one in the basic model, expresses the probability that the devaluation will be of such and such an amount if a formal depreciation decision is made by the government. In the example in Figure 9.4, the devaluation amounts range from 15% to 21%, and the probability of the event is 40%.

The introduction of this kind of probability profile requires some more drastic changes in the model than the previously considered monetary reforms. The following definitions are needed:

Normal fluctuations are the fluctuations of the value of a currency within the support points when no formal devaluation occurs;

Devaluation fluctuations are the changes in the value of a currency as a result of formal parity modifications.

The adaptation of the model will be performed here only in the unitemporal case. In addition to the notation defined in Chapter 2, let a normal fluctuation $= N = S + \tilde{C}_s$, where $S =$ expected amount of the normal fluctuation; and $\tilde{C}_s =$ a variable with a mean of zero and a variance V_s (expressing the uncertainty as to the normal fluctuation amount).

The return on an asset, or the cost of a liability under a wider band proposal, could be expressed as

$$R_i = A + \tilde{C}_i + B_i \tilde{d} D + B_i (1 - \tilde{d}) N$$

The three first terms on the right of the equation are copied directly from Chapter 2, the last term being the only new one. When a devaluation does not occur ($\tilde{d} = 0$), the third term disappears and the last one becomes $+ B_i N$. The normal fluctuations are then affecting the return on the asset or the cost of the liability. In contrast, when a devaluation does occur ($\tilde{d} = 1$), the normal fluctuations disappear and the devaluation fluctuations take over. This value of R_i can be rewritten as follows:

$$R_i = A_i + \tilde{C}_i + B_i[N + \tilde{d}(D - N)]$$

A portfolio of assets and liabilities (that is, a financing and hedging strategy) under wider bands would have a return

$$R = \sum_{i=1}^{N} X_i R_i$$

$$= \sum_{i=1}^{N} X_i(A_i + \tilde{C}_i) + \sum_{i=1}^{N} X_i B_i[N + \tilde{d}(D - N)]$$

$$= \sum_{i=1}^{T} X_i(A_i + \tilde{C}_i) + X_{N+1}[N + \tilde{d}(D - N)]$$

The expected value and the variance of a financing and hedging strategy can be computed as:

$$E = \sum_{i=1}^{N+1} X_i A_i$$

$$V = \sum_{i=1}^{N+1} X_i^2 V_i + \sum_{i=1}^{N} \sum_{j=1}^{N} X_i X_j \, \mathrm{cov}\,(\tilde{C}_i \tilde{C}_j) \qquad i \neq j$$

The optimization model is still

$$\text{maximize } Z = LE - V$$

subject to all operational constraints.

Notice that this model is identical in notation to the basic model of Chapter 2. The only difference is in the meaning of the devaluation coefficient A_{N+1} and the variance of this coefficient V_{N+1}. They are now respectively, the expected value and variance of the term $[N + \tilde{d}(D - N)]$, which are computed as:

$$A_{N+1} = S + P(W - S)$$

$$V_{N+1} = V_s + P[1 - P)(W - S)^2 + V_D - V_S]$$

The potential changes in the present monetary system have now been discussed, and the modifications to the model which would be required by these changes have been developed. In the concluding chapter, a summary of the book is sketched and some possibilities for further research are suggested.

10
Conclusion

This book has shown that extensions of portfolio management theory can solve some important problems in international finance. The key concept is that a strategy can be considered as a "portfolio" of separate decisions over time. The explicit trade-off between risks and expected return (or cost) of different strategies is taken into account.

The key variable of the devaluation-hedging problem is the net exposure. Several transactions allow the treasurer to adjust this key variable to an optimal level by determining a financing and hedging strategy.

The theoretical model has been studied, first on a unitemporal problem, then on a multitemporal problem. A case study showed how a variety of transactions are included in the model.

To make the model operational, some refinements and extensions were discussed. And finally, the operational use of this new tool was described.

Further research is necessary in the devaluation-hedging area. One research topic could be a survey of present practices of companies when they face devaluations. Comparisons with optimal strategy are possible. In contacts with large companies in New York, a wide variety of devaluation-hedging policies and rules of thumb was noticed. One could compare the performance and efficiency of these different practices.

A second research topic could be improvement of predictions of devaluation probabilities and amounts. Recent work has been performed in this area by Paul Einzig, David Zenoff, and Rolf Treuherz.[1] These studies complement each other, but no systematic prediction method applicable in business world conditions has been outlined. Professor Stonehill, from Oregon University, has indicated interest in this topic.

1. See Bibliography.

In summary, the use of operations research techniques in the international finance area is promising. Very little research has been performed up to now in international finance with an operations research approach. The cross-fertilization of these two areas of management could substantially improve current practices in the international financial community.

Mathematical Appendix[1]

Notation:

$$E(\tilde{X}) = \text{expected value of random variable } \tilde{X}.$$
$$\text{cov}\,(\tilde{X}\tilde{Y}) = \text{covariance of random variables } \tilde{X} \text{ and } \tilde{Y}.$$

All other notation is from Chapter 2.

From Chapter 1:

$$R_k = \sum_{i=1}^{N} X_{ik}[A_{ik} + \tilde{C}_{ik} + B_{ik}\tilde{d}_k(W_k + \tilde{C}_{Dk})]$$

$$R_m = \sum_{i=1}^{N} X_{jm}[A_{jm} + \tilde{C}_{jm} + B_{jm}\tilde{d}_m(W_m + \tilde{C}_{Dm})]$$

It is known that

$$E(\tilde{C}_{ik}) = E(\tilde{C}_{jm}) = E(\tilde{C}_{Dk}) = E(\tilde{C}_{Dm}) = 0$$

and that the random variables $\tilde{d}_k$, $\tilde{C}_{Dk}$, $\tilde{C}_{ik}$ are independent and that $\tilde{d}_m$, $\tilde{C}_{Dm}$, $\tilde{C}_{jm}$ are independent; but the pairs $\tilde{d}_k$ and $\tilde{d}_m$, $\tilde{C}_{Dk}$ and $\tilde{C}_{Dm}$, $\tilde{C}_{ik}$ and $\tilde{C}_{jm}$ are *not* independent. By definition

$$\text{cov}\,(R_k R_m) = E[(R_k - E(R_k))(R_m - E(R_m))].$$

Compute

$$E(R_k) = E\left[\sum_{i=1}^{N} X_{ik} A_{ik} + \sum_{i=1}^{N} X_{ik} \tilde{C}_{ik} + \sum_{i=1}^{N} X_{ik} B_{ik} \tilde{d}_k(W_k + \tilde{C}_{Dk})\right]$$

$$= \sum_{i=1}^{N} X_{iK} A_{iK} + X_{N+k} A_{N+k}$$

because $\tilde{d}_k$ and $\tilde{C}_{Dk}$ are independent and $E(\tilde{C}_{ik}) = E(\tilde{C}_{Dk}) = 0$. Therefore,

$$R_k - E(R_k) = \sum_{i=1}^{N} X_{ik} \tilde{C}_{ik} + X_{N+k}[\tilde{d}_k(W_k + \tilde{C}_{Dk}) - A_{N+k}]$$

---

1. This appendix is a direct application of the mathematical appendix on multi-index models in Kalman J. Cohen and Jerry A. Pogue, "An Empirical Evaluation of Alternative Portfolio-Selection Models," *Journal of Business of the University of Chicago* vol. 40, no. 2 (April 1967), pp. 166–193.

and

$$\mathrm{cov}\,(R_d R_m) = [R_k - E(R_k)][R_m - E(R_m)]$$

$$= \left[\sum_{i=1}^{N} X_{ik}\tilde{C}_{ik} + X_{N+k}\tilde{d}_k W_k + X_{N+k}\tilde{d}_k \tilde{C}_{Dk} - X_{N+k}A_{N+k}\right]$$

$$\times \left[\sum_{j=1}^{N} X_{jm}\tilde{C}_{jm} + X_{N+m}\tilde{d}_m W_m + X_{N+m}\tilde{d}_m \tilde{C}_{Dm}\right.$$
$$\left. - X_{N+m}A_{N+m}\right]$$

$$= \sum_{i=1}^{N} X_{ik}\tilde{C}_{ik}\left[\sum_{j=1}^{N} X_{jm}\tilde{C}_{jm} + X_{N+m}\tilde{d}_m W_m\right.$$
$$\left. + X_{N+m}\tilde{d}_m \tilde{C}_{Dm} - X_{N+m}A_{N+m}\right]$$

$$+ X_{N+k}\tilde{d}_k W_k\left[\sum_{j=1}^{N} X_{jm}\tilde{C}_{jm} + X_{N+m}\tilde{d}_m W_m\right.$$
$$\left. + X_{N+m}\tilde{d}_m \tilde{C}_{Dm} - X_{N+m}A_{N+m}\right]$$

$$+ X_{N+k}\tilde{d}_k \tilde{C}_{Dk}\left[\sum_{j=1}^{N} X_{jm}\tilde{C}_{jm} + X_{N+m}\tilde{d}_m W_m\right.$$
$$\left. + X_{N+m}\tilde{d}_m \tilde{C}_{Dm} - X_{N+m}A_{N+m}\right]$$

$$- X_{N+k}A_{N+k}\left[\sum_{j=1}^{N} X_{jm}\tilde{C}_{jm} + X_{N+m}\tilde{d}_m W_m\right.$$
$$\left. + X_{N+m}\tilde{d}_m \tilde{C}_{Dm} - X_{N+m}A_{N+m}\right]$$

By taking the expected value of these terms, one obtains

$$\mathrm{cov}\,(R_k R_m) = \sum_{i=1}^{N} X_{ik}\sum_{j=1}^{N} X_{jm}\,\mathrm{cov}\,(\tilde{C}_{ik}\tilde{C}_{jm})$$
$$+ X_{N+k}X_{N+m}W_k W_m[\mathrm{cov}\,(\tilde{d}_k \tilde{d}_m) + P_k P_m]$$
$$- X_{N+k}X_{N+m}A_{N+k}A_{N+m}$$
$$+ X_{N+k}X_{N+m}\,\mathrm{cov}\,(\tilde{C}_{Dk}\tilde{C}_{Dm})[\mathrm{cov}\,(\tilde{d}_k \tilde{d}_m) + P_k P_m]$$

because

$$E(\tilde{d}_k \tilde{d}_m) = \mathrm{cov}\,(\tilde{d}_k \tilde{d}_m) + P_k P_m$$
$$= \sum_{i=1}^{N} X_{ik}\sum_{j=1}^{N} X_{jm}\,\mathrm{cov}\,(\tilde{C}_{ik}\tilde{C}_{jm}) + X_{N+k}X_{N+m}W_k W_m\,\mathrm{cov}\,(\tilde{d}_k \tilde{d}_m)$$
$$+ X_{N+k}X_{N+m}\,\mathrm{cov}\,(\tilde{C}_{Dk}\tilde{C}_{Dm})[\mathrm{cov}\,(\tilde{d}_k \tilde{d}_m) + P_k P_m]$$

$$= \sum_{i=1}^{N} X_{ik} \sum_{j=1}^{N} X_{jm} \operatorname{cov}(\tilde{C}_{ik} \tilde{C}_{jm})$$

$$+ X_{N+k} X_{N+m} [W_k W_m \operatorname{cov}(\tilde{d}_k \tilde{d}_m) + \operatorname{cov}(\tilde{d}_k \tilde{d}_m) \operatorname{cov}(\tilde{C}_{Dk} \tilde{C}_{Dm})$$

$$+ P_k P_m \operatorname{cov}(\tilde{C}_{Dk} \tilde{C}_{Dm})] \qquad i \neq j$$

The first term,

$$\sum_{i=1}^{N} X_{ik} \sum_{j=1}^{N} X_{jm} \operatorname{cov}(\tilde{C}_{ik} \tilde{C}_{jm}),$$

refers to the correlation of the business risks of the different variables in successive periods. The other term measures the correlation of successive periods owing to correlations of devaluation characteristics.

Define the coefficient of $X_{N+k} X_{N+m}$ as

$$C_{km} = W_k W_m \operatorname{cov}(\tilde{d}_k \tilde{d}_m) + \operatorname{cov}(\tilde{d}_k \tilde{d}_m) \operatorname{cov}(\tilde{C}_{Dk} \tilde{C}_{Dm})$$

$$+ P_k P_m \operatorname{cov}(\tilde{C}_{Dk} \tilde{C}_{Dm}),$$

then,

$$\operatorname{cov}(R_k R_m) = \sum_{i=1}^{N} X_{ik} \sum_{j=1}^{N} X_{jm} \operatorname{cov}(\tilde{C}_{ik} \tilde{C}_{jm}) + X_{N+k} X_{N+m} C_{km} \qquad i \neq j$$

For practical use, only the most important correlations should be included in the model.

Selected Bibliography

Cohen, Gerome B., and Zinbarg, Edward. *Investment Analysis and Portfolio Management*. Homewood, Ill.: Richard D. Irwin, 1967.

Cohen, Kalman, J., and Elton, Edwin T. "Inter-temporal Portfolio Analysis based on Simulations of Joint Returns." *Management Science*, vol. 14, 1 (Sept. 1967), pp. 5–18.

Cohen, Kalman J., and Pogue, Jerry A. "An Empirical Evaluation of Alternative Portfolio-Selection Models." *Journal of Business of the University of Chicago*, vol. 40, no. 2 (April 1967), pp. 166–193.

Dantzig, George Bernard. *Linear Programming and Extensions*. Princeton, N.J.: Princeton University Press, 1963.

de Vries, Margaret G. "The Magnitude of Exchange Devaluation." *Finance and Development*, vol. 5, no. 2 (June 1968), pp. 8–12.

Dorn, W. S. "Duality in Quadratic Programming." *Quarterly of Applied Mathematics*, vol. 18, (Feb. 1960), pp. 155–162.

Einzig, Paul. *The History of Foreign Exchanges*. London: MacMillan Co.; New York: St. Martin's Press, 1962.

Einzig, Paul. *A Textbook on Foreign Exchange*. New York: St. Martin's Press, 1966.

Einzig, Paul. *A Dynamic Theory of Forward Exchange*. 2nd ed. New York: St. Martin's Press, 1967.

Einzig, Paul. *Leads and Lags: The Main Cause of Devaluation*. New York: St. Martin's Press, 1968.

Einzig, Paul. *Foreign Exchange Crisis: An Essay in Economic Pathology*. New York: St. Martin's Press, 1968.

Evitt, Herbert Edwin, and Syrett, W. W. *A Manual of Foreign Exchange*. 6th ed. by W. W. Syrett. London: Pitman Publishing Corporation, 1966.

Farrar, Donald F. *The Investment Decision under Uncertainty*. Englewood Cliffs, N.J.: Prentice-Hall, Inc., 1962.

Hadley, George Francis. *Nonlinear and Dynamic Programming*. Reading, Mass.: Addison-Wesley Publishing Company, 1964.

Hadley, George Francis. *Introduction to Probability and Statistical Decision Theory*. San Francisco: Holden Day, 1967.

Hammersley, J. M., and Handscomb, D. C. *Monte Carlo Methods.* New York: John Wiley & Sons, 1964.

Hertz, David. "Risk Analysis in Capital Investment." *Harvard Business Review*, 42 (Jan.–Feb. 1964), pp. 95–106.

Hillier, Frederick Stanton. "The Derivation of Probabilistic Information for the Evaluation of Risky Investments." *Management Science*, vol 9, no. 3 (April 1963), pp. 443–457.

Hillier, Frederick Stanton, and Lieberman, Gerald J. *Introduction to Operations Research.* San Francisco: Holden Day, 1967.

Lietaer, Bernard A. " Managing Risks in Foreign Exchange." *Harvard Business Review* (March–April 1970), pp. 127–138.

Markowitz, Harry M. "Portfolio Selection." *The Journal of Finance*, vol. 7, no. 1 (March 1952), pp. 77–91.

Markowitz, Harry M. "The Optimization of a Quadratic Function subject to Linear Constraints." *Naval Research Logistics Quarterly*, vol. 3 (March–June 1956), pp. 111–133.

Markowitz, Harry M. *Portfolio Selection: Efficient Diversification of Investments.* Cowles Foundation Monograph No. 16. New York: John Wiley & Sons, 1959.

Orgler, Yair. "An Unequal-Period Model for Cash Management by Business Firms." Paper presented at the TIMS/ORSA Joint Meeting, San Francisco, Calif., May 1968.

Pack, L. *Optimale Bestellmenge und Optimale Lossgröbe-Zu Einigen Problemen ihrer Ermittlung* (Wiesbaden, 1964).

Pogue, Jerry A. "An Adaptive Model for Investment Management." Ph.D. Thesis, Carnegie Institute of Technology, July 1967.

Reimann, Guenter, and Wigglesworth, Edwin, F. *The Challenge of International Finance.* New York: McGraw-Hill, 1966.

Robichek, Alexander A., and Meyer, Stewart C. *Optimal Financing Decisions.* Englewood Cliffs, N.J.: Prentice-Hall, Inc., 1965.

Robichek, Alexander A., Teichrow, D., and Jones, J. M. "Optimal Short-Term Financing Decisions." *Management Science*, vol. 12, no. 1 (Sept. 1965), pp. 1–36.

Sharpe, William. "A Simplified Model for Portfolio Analysis." *Management Science*, vol. 9, no. 2 (January 1963), pp. 277–293.

C. H. Springer, et al. *Probabilistic Models*, Vol. 4 of Mathematics for Management Series. Homewood, Ill.: Richard D. Irwin, Inc., 1968.

Tobin, James. "Liquidity Preferences as Behavior Toward Risk." *Review of Economic Studies*, vol. 25, no. 68, (February 1958).

Treuherz, Rolf M. "Forecasting Foreign Exchange Rates in Inflationary Economics." *Financial Executive* (February 1969), vol. 38, no. 2, pp. 57–60.

Van Horne, J. *Financial Management and Policy.* Englewood Cliffs, N.J.: Prentice-Hall, Inc., 1968.

Villanueva, Marta. "Information Systems under Inflation." Unpublished working paper at the M.I.T. Sloan School of Management, 1968.

Weingartner, Martin H. "Capital Budgeting of Interrelated Projects: a survey and synthesis." *Management Science*, vol. 12, no. 7 (March 1966), pp. 485–516.

Weingartner, Martin H. *Mathematical Programming and the Analysis of Capital Budgeting Problems.* Englewood Cliffs, N.J.: Prentice-Hall, Inc., 1963.

Wolfe, Philip. "The Simplex Method for Quadratic Programming." *Econometrica*, vol. 27, no. 3 (July 1959), pp. 382–390.

Zangwill, Willard I. "The Convex Simplex Method." *Management Science*, vol. 14, no. 3 (November 1967), pp. 221–238.

Zenoff, David. "Environmental Forecasting is a Tricky Business." *Worldwide P & I Planning.* (September-October 1968), pp. 20–27.

Index

Bernouilli, Daniel, 32
Bonds: hedging, 82–83, 92–94, 96–
100; "mythical" (measuring the
subjective value of profit remittances), 84; regular, 8, 16, 28, 30–
31, 47–51, 53, 56–57, 64–65, 81, 83,
92–95, 97–101, 110, 139–140
Brealey, Richard A., 15 n
Bretton Woods agreement, 143

Capital budgeting, 53, 116, 117–120,
128, 149
Cash, 5, 8, 10–11, 26–29, 39, 44–45,
47, 49–50, 56–57, 59, 62, 64–67,
69–70, 73–75, 79, 81–82, 85, 89–90,
97, 113, 117, 119, 136, 139–140,
142; flow, 36, 45, 51, 56–57, 59, 67,
70, 72–74, 79, 82, 97, 114, 117–
119; requirements, 6, 45, 50, 56, 97,
100, 116, 118; requirements, basic,
57–59, 64, 96, 136.
Chebyshev's inequality, 14
Cohen, Gerome B., 110 n
Cohen, Kalman J., 22 n
Constraints: general and various operational, 2, 8, 10–11, 38, 41, 45–
46, 52–53, 56, 64–67, 69–70, 74–75,
79–81, 85, 89 n, 90–91, 102, 111–
115, 119, 128, 135, 137, 142, 145,
147 n, 149, 154; maximum or minimum, 8, 35–36, 47, 51, 68–70, 76,
79–82, 85, 90, 115, 119, 128–129,
137, 142; policy, 8, 11, 25–26, 46,
56, 68–69, 82, 84, 90
Correlation, 10–11, 22–24, 27–29, 32,
40, 42, 46, 55–56, 102–110, 118,
119 n, 126, 136–37, 146–48; between asset and liability variables,
22–24, 109–110; correlation of de-

valuation data between currencies,
146–148; of devaluation probabilities and amounts, 40, 42, 46, 55–
56, 103–108, 136. *See also* Covariance
Correlation matrices, 105, 108
Cost, 2, 6–12, 14, 17, 19, 22, 26, 29,
32, 38, 40, 43, 45–48, 50–51, 54,
56–58, 62, 64–70, 72, 75, 78–80, 82,
85–87, 89–90, 92, 94, 96, 99–102,
109, 113–114, 120, 122–129, 131,
133–134, 137, 140–142, 153; maximum possible cost, 137; most likely
cost, 137. *See also* Losses; Interest
Covariance, 11 n, 22–25, 29, 39–42,
56, 109, 118, 124, 130, 137, 146–
149, 154; of risk over time, 39;
term introduction, "devaluation covariance," 39. *See* Mathematical
Appendix for definitions, 157–159.
See also Correlation
Crawling peg proposal, 144, 151–152

Dantzig, George Bernard, 9 n
Decision theory, statistical, 2
Decision variables, 57, 59, 74–76, 92,
96–97, 103, 116, 124–127, 136, 148
Decisions: contingent, 103, 115, 117–
118; general financing and hedging,
7, 9–10, 12, 15, 33, 38, 46–47, 50,
56–57, 113, 116–117, 120, 130, 133,
142, 155; mutually exclusive, 103,
114–115, 117–118; policy, 11, 68,
90
Deflationary policies, 104
Depreciation. *See* Devaluation
Devaluation, 2–11, 13–25, 28–30, 34,
37–42, 45–46, 48, 50–56, 59, 61–65,
72–73, 76–78, 82, 85–86, 89, 96–97,